CONFRONTING THE ENEMY

A Journey Into Spiritual Warfare

by

Dr. Steven L. Bennett

Prologue

The physical world in which we live allows us to see things as they **seem** to be. The spirit world is the **real** world. There is a world that exists beyond the one that is seen. This is illustrated in 2 Kings 6:17 when God opened the eyes of the young man to see beyond what seemed to be true and to look into the reality of the spirit world. The darkness in the spirit world is very subtle in its creep into the lives, cultures, and nations of men. The enemy, as he manifests himself, usually poses as another entity to be seen rather than himself. People will simply surmise that it is culture, politics, certain leaders, etc. that propagate darkness when, in fact, it is the kingdom of Satan behind the wickedness in the created world.

I once heard a popular Christian teacher say on the radio that there is nothing a believer can do to affect the demonic world. When I heard him say that, my first impression was that he had never been on the front lines of spiritual warfare and he was overlooking a world of scriptures to reach that conclusion. I could never follow someone who knows more than he has experienced on a Biblical basis.

This darkness is seldom bothered by Christians who have resigned themselves to simply accommodate the darkness and to try living alongside it. They coexist with the dark kingdom while "having church" or "doing church" .The clash of kingdoms takes place when Christians decide to "be the church" and displace darkness with light. This will always require a battle as Satan does not give up ground without a fight.

When I first began to realize that we are in a war for the souls of men, and I came face to face with the real enemy, hell was unleashed with a fury right before my eyes. This entire subject frightens some, interests others, and will be rejected by many. It is an ugly, filthy reality that must be faced when the enemy must be confronted. The kingdom of Satan is nasty, reptilian, and dark.

My baptism into the darkness of the spirit world came out of a powerful revival that I have written about in a book called **Walking In The Wind**. It was a move of God as I had never experienced before. When I found myself confronted with the ugly darkness of the spirit world, I had to rethink everything principle of demonization that I had embraced up to that point. I was forced to rethink theology, how to bind the enemy's power, learn what it is to be an overcomer, and how to exercise the spiritual authority of Jesus. What follows are the observations of one who has been on the front lines of battle against hell's forces and has seen the enemy face to face. It does not come from something read in a book, but rather out of the overflow of an intense time in my ministry. What an astounding reality was mine when "greater is He who is in me..." became my refuge.

My hope is that I never have to delve into this world again but if it means tearing down the strongholds of darkness in order to capture the souls of men for heaven, I stand ready.

Manifestations
Chapter 1

For many weeks, there was a spirit of brokenness, prayer, and worship on our church. In standing against the darkness, we had seen God do literal miracles outside the walls of our church. While we were doing battle for our community, there was also a rash of internal manifestations of the demonic. I had dealt with demonic situations before but never on this level. We were entering a new world of warfare that I had only read about in missionary accounts. I had to rethink my theology, who I was in Christ, under what authority I labored, and how to be more than a conqueror in the power of His might.

Strange events began to happen within our church buildings. These were harmless events but yet distracting. For an example, there were several wooden doors leading into our sanctuary. One of these doors developed an odor that smelled like urine. Our housekeeper scrubbed the door. Within twenty-four hours, the odor had returned. More scrubbing took place with stronger cleansers. The odor returned. One of our men removed the door from its hinges and sanded it down to its wooden veneer. He reapplied the sealer and rehung the door. Within twenty-four hours, the odor returned. Eventually we had to replace the entire unit in order to be free of the smell.

We also played "cat and mouse" with lights in the building. When the lights were turned off at the end of a day, some were back on again before the custodian could get home. It was like bad children were playing tricks on the church staff. This went on for a very long time. I am not sure if we ever had all the lights out at one time again before we sold the building. I had experienced this in another church once and recognized the source.

There were other distractions but most were harmless. The real battle was just ahead. When the demonic began manifesting in our people, we moved into a new world of warfare.

The Sunday morning service was almost over. Kenny was singing the last song of the morning as a solo. To seek God, many were still filling the altars. One of the young men who sang on our praise team stepped down to the altar to pray. Many were already in the altar.

As he knelt down, for some reason one of our pastors standing nearby stepped forward and put a hand on him and prayed, "I plead the blood of Jesus over this one".

Hell was unleashed at that moment. The young man growled like a wounded bear. There were four other men who lay draped over the altar praying. The young man lifted it completely off the ground with one hand. Another one of our pastors immediately stepped down in an attempt to control the situation so that people would not be afraid. As the pastor stepped down, the troubled young man grabbed the pastor's tie and almost broke his neck. Ties were never worn again while dealing with the demonized. I was seated on the platform but when I noticed what was happening, I had a witness in my spirit of what it was. I quickly stepped down, took authority over the spirit, and bound it up to quieten it.

All afternoon we received calls of frightened people asking about the incident. Declaring that we no longer were doing God's work but rather were involved in radical things, some longtime members never returned and joined other churches. We didn't try to dissuade them.

To deal with this situation, we made an appointment for the next evening with the troubled young man. I had twenty-four hours to equip myself to deal directly with the demonic. Many questions filled my mind. My theology warred with spiritual reality. This young man had professed Christ since childhood. He had been much involved with youth ministry, worship, and now, adult ministry. I was always taught that a believer could not be demonized, but here was one that seemed to be.

Three of our pastors and I met with this young man on Monday night at 7:00 o'clock. I loved this young man and desperately wanted to see him set free. We sat in my office and I asked him to close his eyes and not to respond to anything that I said or asked. He bowed with closed eyes and I began.

"In the name of Jesus Christ, the Son of God who died on Calvary's cross, I command you to identify yourself."

Silence. I wondered if I would be able to confront the enemy adequately. I knew that I had been given the authority of Jesus to trample over snakes and scorpions and over all the power of the enemy (Luke 10:19) and was standing in that authority. Once again I told the young man not to respond to me. I spoke again.

"By the power of the shed blood of Jesus Crist of Nazareth, I order you to identify yourself to me. I am your conqueror in Jesus' name."

A twitch of the cheek. I knew at that moment that we were pressuring the wicked spirit. I continued.

"I am your conqueror in Jesus Christ and Jesus is your Lord. I command you to identify yourself."

A cynical laugh came from the young man.

"You have no power over me. He is mine," a guttural voice spat out.

"I don't have power over you, but the Spirit of God in me has all power over you (Matthew 12:28) and you must leave."

Again, a cynical laugh. The room was cold; there was an eerie atmosphere.

"Let's talk in French." A cynical laugh.

"I will not allow you speak in French. You will speak to me in English. You are going to leave this man. You have no choice. This is the will of God and I am speaking in His authority. He came to destroy your works, and you will not stay."

"Hey, can we take a break? Call your mama. She needs to talk to you."

"I will not accept any response from you except for your submission to the authority of Jesus in me. You must leave now and never come back."

"I am not going. He wants me to stay."

"You are a liar. The truth is that you are a defeated spirit and have no rights in this man. I take back the grounds you think that you have in him and place his life under the complete Lordship of Jesus Christ."

"He doesn't want me to leave. I will stay because he wants me to."

"Is that the truth?"

"Yessss."

Silence.

"Will that stand as truth before the throne of the Living God?"

Silence.

"I command you to respond in truth. Am I your conqueror in Jesus Christ?"

Squirming and twitching.

"Answer me now, in English."

"Yessssss!!"

"Say it out loud. Say, 'You are my conqueror in Jesus Christ.'"

"You are my conqueror but I will not say His name."

The spirit threw the young man to the floor and he slithered like a snake toward an exterior door in my office that led to the parking lot.

"Stop. In the name of Jesus, be still!"

The slithering stopped. I had a solemn realization at this point. I was speaking to a spirit being that had his beginning before the worlds were formed. He had been working wickedness as long as man had been upon the earth.

"Why won't you say His name?"

Silence. Twitching.

"You know Him don't you? You once worshiped Him before His throne."

" Yessss," he said remorsefully.

"But then you followed your idiot leader and will pay the eternal consequence in hell."

Screaming with nasty, slobbering anger.

"Be still and be quiet!" I was on my knees leaning over him on the floor. I happened to lay my Bible on his back unintentionally. He screamed like it burned him.

"Get it off!!"

"This is the truth of God, isn't it?"

"Yesssss."

"This truth says that I have the authority of Jesus and you must obey me. I command you to leave."

"I won't leave. I have no place to go."

"Then if you have no place to go, by the finger of God I send you to the pit to be bound until you are judged."

A shriek. "NO!"

"Go now. Leave and go to the place I am sending you."

There was a hair-raising shriek that tore at the young man on the floor. The scream sounded like it fell into a well and diminished as it left.

The young man looked at me with fear in his eyes. I cradled his head in my lap.

"I love you," I said. "You are free. He won't be back. Jesus is Lord in your life again."

I never knew this spirit's name. We had dealt with him for an hour and a half.

The next day, one of our families asked about the session that took place in my office. They were in their living room in their house across the street from the church when they heard the spirit scream. They were not sure what was going on at the church but they knew that it was serious.

I was sick for a week with congestion, coughing, and sinus pain. I did not know it then but this would be a pattern. Every spirit I dealt with caused me to be sick afterward just from the nasty spiritual debris that surrounded them. It would happen every time after a deliverance experience.

Like a Flood
Chapter 2

The call came at 2:00 in the morning. When my phone rang I knew it wasn't going to be good. The woman on the other end of the line said frantically, "Preacher, we need you right now!"

"What in the world is going on?" I asked sleepily.

"It's Chuck. He is destroying the house."

"Is he drunk?"

"No, he is just out of control. Me and the children are frightened and don't know what to do. Wayne and Brian (friends from church) are here also but they don't know what to do."

"Why don't you just call the sheriff's department? They can settle your husband down."

"No, please, we need you. We don't know how to handle this," she cried.

"I will be there in about twenty minutes," I wearily said.

I got out of bed, dressed, and drove to their home. When I arrived and walked into the house, the mother and children were huddled together in the kitchen with panic in their eyes. Wayne and Brian were in the hallway on their knees praying outside of a closed bedroom door. The house looked like a storm had passed through it.

I walked down the hallway to where Brian was kneeling with a frightened look on his face. Wayne was standing there also.

Jim said, "I'm glad you are here; we aren't sure of what to do."

"So, what is happening?" I asked.

"It's Chuck. He is in a rage, tearing the house apart and growling like an animal."

I knew in my spirit at that point what we were dealing with. I put my hand on the knob to open the bedroom door.

Brian spoke quickly, "Are you going in there?"

"I don't know any other way to settle this than to go in and handle it," I replied.

"We are going to stay out here and pray, if that's ok", he quickly volunteered.

When I opened the door, the room was dark because the ceiling fan with its three lights had been ripped from the ceiling. The bed had been turned over and lay against the wall. Other articles were scattered around the small room. The street light was streaming in through sheer curtains, and Chuck stood as a silhouette against the outside light. He was standing barefoot on the broken glass on the floor. He was breathing heavily with a slight moan or growl under his breath. A spiritual antagonism rose within my spirit.

"What ARE you doing?" I asked in exasperation.

He stood with only his underwear on.

"I will kill you," he threatened.

This man was my friend and we had had many discussions in the past several years. I had been in his home several times.

"You not only aren't going to kill me; you will not destroy anything else in this house." I told him.

"And who do you think is going to stop me? You?" he sneered.

I knew I was not talking to my friend. I stepped up nose to nose with him, his fists clenched on each side. His breathing became labored and quick.

"In the name of Jesus Christ, who shed His blood on the cross and defeated you, I take authority over you and command you to be still and quiet."

"You have no authority over me; I will kill you," he threatened again.

I faced him down, backing him up as I spoke. The disgust of the Holy Spirit rose within me.

"You will settle down and yield control of this man. The authority of Jesus stands with me and you know you must," I said as I backed him up.

He backed into the turned over mattress on the floor. I stayed nose to nose with him, angry at what this spirit was doing to my friend and his family.

"You no longer have authority or control. I am in charge now by the power of the Living God."

He backed until he fell backward across the mattress. I stayed in his face demanding his submission.

When he could move no more but lay back on the mattress, he blinked in the filtered light of the street lamp.

"Preacher?" he said in a confused voice.

"Chuck, it is going to be ok. We will deal with this and you won't be bothered anymore", I assured him.

He touched me on my shoulder. I helped him up and out of the room. He was again the friend I had known; however, a demonic presence had manifested itself in another believer.

We agreed to meet in my office the next night and get to the bottom of this.

When Chuck spoke to me the next night in the presence of several of our pastors, he revealed the grounds that he had surrendered to Satan in his life and we discovered the legal reasons why the demonic felt welcome to control him. In repentance, he renounced the past sins that had opened his life to these spirits.

As before, I asked him to close his eyes and refrain from speaking to me or answering my questions. He bowed his head with eyes closed.

"I am your conqueror in Jesus' name. I want you to tell me who you are," I spoke in the authority of God.

Silence.

I refused to accept the silence.

"You will speak to me and tell me who you are, by the power of the cross", I repeated.

Chuck shivered, twitched, and spoke in a voice different from the one I was used to in my friend.

"My name is Power. I am the strongest power here. You have no power over me," he snarled.

"You know that is a lie and you are like your leader Satan, who is the father of lies. I don't accept your power because all power in heaven and earth has been given to Jesus Who allows me to use His authority to release this one from your power", I spoke forcefully.

A shiver and a separate voice muttered. I realized in my spirit that we were not dealing with only one spirit but several. As pastors, we would come to refer to this condition as an MCI (multiple critter infestation) in later experiences.

"I want to talk to the one in charge", I said.

Silence.

"I won't accept your silence. You must identify yourself. I want to speak to the one in charge. Tell me who you are," I demanded.

"I am here," the spirit spoke.

"What is your name?" I demanded again.

"I don't have a name," he said.

"What do you have to do with this man?" I inquired.

"I hold the door open for the others to come and go," he confessed.

"What other ones? Tell me with truth that will stand before the throne of God as truth", I instructed.

"They are called "the faceless ones", he said.

I had a picture in my mind of honey bees working around a hive, coming and going as this one held the door opened for them.

"Are you in charge?" I asked.

Silence.

"I command you to tell me if you are in charge," I spoke.

"No, I am not in charge," he said.

I later learned that the leader will hide in an attempt to escape expulsion.

"I want to talk to the one in charge and no one else. Being your authority, I demand that you identify yourself," I said with agitation.

"I'm here," he muttered.

"What is your name?"

"I am Dominion. I am in charge and will stay in charge. He is mine," he growled.

"You are no longer in charge; I am in charge by the power of the Spirit of God. You will do as I say. You are going to leave and never come back. You cannot stay. I am reclaiming this life for the Lordship of Jesus Christ," I declared.

He wanted to argue and reason. He was good with words. Knowing that all he could do was to lie and deceive, I refused to discuss anything with this spirit. He would do anything to distract from the real mission at that moment. I knew that if I could make him leave, the others would go also.

After an hour of demanding and refusing, I finally forced him to begin to speak the truth of scripture. He hated that. It dislodged him a little more with each confession of truth.

"Is Jesus your Lord?" I asked.

"Yesssss," with an angry growl.

"Say it, Jesus is my Lord." I demanded.

"I won't say it."

"Am I your conqueror in Jesus Christ?" I asked.

"Yessssss."

"Say it; I am your conqueror in Jesus Christ. By the authority of Christ you say it." I spoke in commanding language.

"You are my authority in Him," he confessed. He would not speak the Lord's name.

"By that authority, I command that you confess that Jesus Christ is your Lord," I demanded.

There was a cough and heaving. I told one of the pastors to grab the trash can. I knew it was going to be nasty. Before they could get the trash can to me, I caught a double handful of mucous in my cupped hands as the spirits were torn from him. This would become a pattern with each experience of deliverance. They would vomit, empty their sinuses, or burp loudly as the spirits left.

Chuck lifted his eyes to mine and a peaceful smile began to break on his countenance.

"Are you free?" I asked.

With joy he replied, "I am free."

Chuck continues to celebrate this date each year as his time of deliverance. Both of those young children, who huddled in the kitchen with their mother that frightening night, are now leaders and servants in their church with children of their own.

I was sick for three weeks after this session.

Multiple Battlegrounds
Chapter 3

As individuals continued to manifest the demonic in their lives, word began to leak out that our pastors were knowledgeable enough to deal with demonization. When that word was passed about, people outside of our church began to contact us for help with themselves, spouses, children, and friends. I did not want to develop a "deliverance ministry" simply because the Bible does not demonstrate that as a calling. As with Jesus, Paul, and others in the scriptures, they dealt with the demonic as the need arose but went about spreading the gospel after dealing with it. Still, we helped some related to our church in some way.

As we were approached by individuals, we learned to diagnose symptoms of personal demonization. Some people are just naturally strange. If they were hearing voices, losing control of areas of their life, having blank times when they didn't remember the passing of that time, seeing things that weren't there, suffering personality changes momentarily, or other unexplained behaviors, we agreed to help them come to freedom. Not all were demonized.

We met with a young man who suffered a turbulent growing up period with much rebellion, rejection by his parents, and dabbling in sinful behavior. A spirit who called himself Judas was the strong one who shouted, "I own him". In all, we identified thirteen named spirits integrated into his life.

There was the Evangelist who had been troubled for a very long time. In his teenage years he had opened up doors that gave legal grounds for the demonic to control areas of his life. While we identified a dozen spirits by name, the interesting one was the spirit that took on the name of Jesus. It was then that I realized that not everything done in the name of Jesus refers to God's only Son. Another spirit that was very difficult to dislodge from his life was only dispensed with through worshiping God out loud in his presence. Some of or pastors sang praise music as I dealt with the spirit. He could not stand the exaltation of Jesus in the worship and left.

Les was a young man that had been caught up in much darkness and now had committed his life Christ. That only stirred up a hornet's nest of demonic activity. We identified thirty-one named spirits in his life. It was a difficult session that lasted for hours.

There was also the pastor's son who was married with children but had suffered a lot of loneliness and rejection from his father. The father took part in some dark cultural events that opened up a door on the whole family to be bothered by the demonic. Freedom came after some difficult wrestling with the controlling forces.

There was the teenaged girl who was controlled by a sensuous spirit. It manifested in the presence of our pastors who were dealing with it. When the father was called to come into the meeting, the spirit left because of the father's covering over his daughter.

My wife and I also saw demonic manifestation in a child not quite two years old. When I got near to the child being held by her mother, the child locked eyes with me and I knew there was evil there. This spirit would not let us pray for the child without screaming and interrupting. The child had been subjected to occult type forces by a spiritual leader in an effort to help it. The door had been opened.

We not only were forced to deal with situations where people had personal manifestations but we learned that darkness was also revealing itself on multiple fronts.

We found that when the Holy Spirit was especially active in our worship services that some people could not stay in the services with God's presence so strong. A middle aged woman left the service at times and went into the restroom to vomit when the presence of the Holy Spirit was strong in the service. Her mother had been involved in witchcraft and occult practices. There was also the teenaged boy who also left the services during intense time to throw up in the bathroom and then to lose control of his personality, lay writhing on the floor, and making strange noises in the hallway of the church building. It was not unusual for some to leave the powerful times of worship.

Another front that we were forced to deal with was the presence of darkness manifesting in the homes of our people. As we dealt with the demonic and I taught on spiritual warfare, happenings in homes began to make sense to them. Strange things would happen in houses but they didn't realize until now what the source of the weirdness was. My wife and I had unusual events happen in our house.

Jack was a young pastor with a wife and small children. I had known him for several years and he was a casual friend. He sat with me and told me his story one morning. In the house that he was renting he began to notice unexplainable events. His infant child woke up many nights screaming in fear and refusing to go back to sleep in her room. She was too young to talk and speak of what the problem was. The pastor put a tape player in her room and played soft worship music as the child dozed off peacefully. In the night he and his wife were awakened by an awful noise. He jumped from his bed and ran to his baby's room only to find that the tape player had been jammed into the attic fan in the hallway. He also noticed that his arm was dripping blood running to the ends of his fingers but he had done nothing to injure himself. He and his wife also began to see apparitions and sense the presence of beings in certain rooms of their home.

There was Alfred who asked me to come to his house and tell him what was going on. He had just gone through a divorce and was emotionally fragile. I went to his home but could not determine anything that would cause dark spirits to feel welcome. When we walked outside, I noticed that the house was built upon a berm that made it stand taller than other houses in the area. I asked him if he knew why that berm was under his house. He told me that the house was built upon an Indian burial ground. That explained some events to me. Several months later, Alfred's body was found in an isolated part of the woods behind his house. No one was ever able to determine what had happened to him.

    People began to tell of seeing children in the hallways of their home. One told of a woman that walked from room to room dressed in the fashion of the 1800's. Some heard voices speaking, items being thrown from cabinets or falling off of the wall. Several had feelings of suicide to find out later that the previous owner had committed suicide.

    We prayed over and sanctified many homes. We taught our people to do the same if they were in doubt about happenings in their house. Most were successful in ending the dark happenings;

some were never able to succeed in ridding their house of these spirits.

When the darkness came against us, it confronted us on many fronts. It seemed that while God was doing some powerful works in the body of our church, we were never free from warfare.

Who is Satan?
Chapter 4

A Biblical look into Satan's background helps the believer better understand the enemy and his strategies. 2 Corinthians 2:11 exhorts us to not be ignorant of the devil's devices. A panoramic view of the army of the enemy would be overwhelming if not for a clear understanding that he is presently already defeated. It is important to be careful of extremism and one must strike a balance of truth and sanity in dealing with supernatural darkness. There is a lot of passed on ignorance that is propagated with no foundation in Biblical truth but rather focused on the sensational.

A common question is "Why did God make the devil?" The skinny answer is that God didn't make the devil; He created a beautiful angelic being named Lucifer and Lucifer became the devil by his own sin. As many know, Satan began his existence as a created angel (Ezekiel 37:13, 15). He was brilliant, beautiful and powerful. Ezekiel 37 gives us a description of his beauty. His name, Lucifer, means "Daystar" and he is called "Son of the Morning" and "Son of the dawn" (Isaiah 14:12). His name parallels those of Jesus. It is thought that he was one of three arch angels, joining with Michael and Gabriel. Ezekiel 37:14 indicates that he was involved in music before the throne of God. To cover the throne with music that inspired worship would explain his desire to be worshiped and how he uses the power of music in his quest against the Kingdom of God. He had access to the very presence of God, and, according to the first chapter of Job, may still have that privilege for a while.

The first sin committed was in heaven when Lucifer rebelled against God and led one third of the angels into the rebellion. A panoramic view of this action is helpful in understanding the sequence of events that led to the present-day alignment of darkness.

Lucifer's fall from his position in heaven was based on his rebellious will. The first sin was one of will and continues to be a stronghold of sin. There is no indication of violence or arms against God, rather simply a clash of wills, it was an act of the heart. In Isaiah's record of Lucifer's fall (Isaiah 14:12-15), "I will" is used by Lucifer five times. While we normally say that Lucifer was "cast out" of heaven, it is more accurate to say that he simply lost his position in heaven since he still seems to have some access on a limited basis to the presence of God (Job 1). The only real loss that he suffered was his position and his holiness. He retained his power, beauty, and power to deceive as did other angels. He remains second in power only to God. His fall is estimated to have happened somewhere between the creation of the world and the creation of Adam and Eve (Job 38:4-7). According to Isaiah 45:18, God created the world perfectly to be inhabited. It was in perfect order and balance. When Satan began to make the earth his domain and took up residence, sin became his goal and chaos then began to infiltrate the earth's perfect setting. Romans 8:21-22 indicates that all of creation groans under the weight of sin.

The earth became his favorite realm. He took Jesus to a high mountain and showed him all the kingdoms of the world and insinuated that he owned them all. He claimed the right of possession to them (Matthew 4:8-9). Jesus did not refute or challenge this. Satan is Biblically referred to as the god of this world (2 Corinthians 4:4). When God created Adam, He gave Adam authority to rule over all of creation (Genesis 1:28). When Adam sinned against God, the ruling scepter given to him was stolen by Satan and will remain so until Jesus drives him out (John 12:31). The first Adam lost it and the second Adam will take it back. He has usurped authority over a stolen kingdom and offered it back to Jesus in exchange for being worshiped.

The rebellion of Satan in heaven is described in Revelation 12:9-10. Verse 4 details that one third of the angels were also banished from heaven in the rebellion. Michael, the archangel, fought against Lucifer and prevailed. In the last days, Satan will be bound and finally cast into hell (Revelation 20:1-4). Jude indicates that some demons (fallen angels) are already in hell (Jude 6). We know that originally, hell was made for the devil and his angels (Matthew 25:41).

A question that seems unsettling to many is, if God is going to banish Satan to hell eventually, why does he wait? Of course, no one knows the mind of God on this but there are some possible answers. Revelation 3:21 identifies overcomers as those who will sit and rule with Him on His throne. Overcomers need an enemy in order to be overcomers. The continuing battle allows the believer to qualify themselves as more than conquerors. God has also used this fallen time to gather to

Himself a people who have committed themselves to Him in spite of the darkness. Perhaps one day we will understand all things He does.

What Are Demons?
Chapter 5

These fallen spirits have been in existence since angels were created. They saw the creation of the universe. They are eternal beings that were present when Adam and Eve were placed in the garden. They have seen history and time unfold.

In one session of dealing with a demonic spirit in the life of a teenager, one of the pastors with me was observing and listening to the demon speak through the voice of the young man. I reminded the demon that he had once worshiped God in heaven before he followed Lucifer and he acknowledge that fact. After this session, this pastor was so taken by the fact that he had been in the presence of a spirit being that had seen the world created, he said that he had questions about the early earth that he wanted to ask one of them. I refused to allow that. Receiving information from a demonic spirit is divination and is prohibited by God. Actually, nothing that a demonic spirit says can be believed anyway since they are masters at lying and deceit.

Hebrews 12:22 identifies that number of angels as "innumerable". One third of an innumerable number is still an innumerable number. Revelation 5:11 paints a picture of so great a number that they cannot be counted. Daniel 7:10 numbers them into the millions. It is not possible to know how many fallen angels there are that are free to do their leader's bidding. Demons are simply angels that have gone bad by following Lucifer's rebellion against God.

The demonic, fallen angels are highly organized, mobile, and very powerful. They are regimented like an army into different levels of authority and responsibility. They are entirely spirit beings, intentionally filthy and wicked. They are living and eternal beings who are ageless, sexless, and degreed in their ranks. There is no Biblical reference of a single one ever dying.

These demonic spirits seem to take on the names of the sin that they produce or the tasks they are given. This is one of the difficulties in identifying them on occasions because the malady they cause seems so "natural". The Bible names various demonic spirits by the work that they do. Here is a list of some: spirits of fear, foul spirits, spirits of error, perverse spirits, unclean spirits, spirits of jealousy, seducing spirits, spirits of whoredom, lying spirits, spirits of infirmity, familiar spirits, deceiving spirits, scheming spirits, dumb spirits, deaf spirits, evil spirits, spirits of divination and others. These spirits are active in murder, suicide, destruction, oppression, accusation, depression, malice, perversion, immorality, hatred, blasphemy, and the occult. They are reptilian in nature and vile in their work.

The work that these demons do in humans is divided into three areas according to the three parts of a human makeup as God created us.

The **emotions** are vulnerable to attack and deception. Fear, hate, resentment, anger, discouragement, despair, and depression are some of the common areas of their work.

The **mind** is the most common arena of warfare. They will attempt to control or influence thinking. Unbelief, doubt, guilt, confusion, spiritual blindness, forgetfulness, schizophrenia, depression, fantasy, defeat, deception, and confusion are some of the manifestations of their mental influence. They cause stinking thinking.

The **body** is also a target of these foul spirits. Not every physical problem or ailment is demonic in nature. Some of our physical problems are simply the result of living in a fallen and dying world. The physical attacks that the demonic may bring have as a goal the destruction of the body. Disease, suicide, sinful indulgences, and murder are some of the works that they do.

In order for the demonic spirits to have access to control in one's life, there must be a point of entry or a legal ground for them to control areas of life. In order for deliverance and freedom to take place, these open doors should be identified and closed by confession, repentance, and renunciation once known.

A common area of entry is through immorality. This includes sexual perversion, promiscuous behavior, adultery, fornication, homosexuality, bestiality, and other forms of sexual sin. These can be opened up to one's life through sexual abuse, pornography, participation, and fantasy. The internet is giving rise to a brand new addicted population. It is readily available in the privacy of a home. I know of a man whose wife became demonized through behaviors that she adopted. It was not long before he also became demonized simply because the demonic can be sexually transmitted. 1 Corinthians 6:16 warns that one who has sex with a prostitute has become one with her and therefore subject to every demonic influence in the prostitute. The message is dire in its warning to "flee sexual immorality" (v. 18) so as to protect one's self from possible demonization.

Another area of concern is found in relationships. How we act and react to each other can determine whether we have placed our self in spiritual danger. A dominating and controlling parent or spouse can spawn anger in one through which the demonic may see as an open door of invitation. This kind of getting control of someone else is akin to witchcraft, which attempts to dominate others. This behavior can result in weak-willed, insecure, and indecisive people who may not be able to stand against the forces seeking to destroy them.

Addictions and compulsive behavior opens doors for controlling spirits to enter one's life. Any behavior that can no longer be controlled may be a standing invitation to spiritual domination. Not all addicts are demonized. Alcohol, drugs, gluttony, gambling, sex and other compulsions makes one vulnerable. These compulsions usually find their roots somewhere else besides the abuse itself. The roots may be tied to fear, unhappiness, response to abuse, and other mental maladies. Sometimes a branch can be cut off of the tree of compulsion and another may grow in its place. One may be able to give up alcohol only to find that overeating, overspending, or over sexing takes its place. The axe must be laid at the root of the tree (Luke 3:9).

A rising area of demonization comes from participation in the occult. It is no longer simply Ouija boards, tarot cards, horoscopes, etc. that is a problem, but new avenues have opened up with computers and gaming. It all seems innocent and only games but there should be no deceit, what is a contradiction of God is sin and an open door for deep spiritual problems.

Music is one of the most powerful forces on earth. Spiritual music is one of the only things that we will take to heaven with us. Music can instantly bring one back to a time in the past or call up forgotten feelings. Most of what we learn through music is never forgotten. Do you still sing the alphabet song in your head in order to place letters in the correct order? Some of today's secular music is dedicated to the occult and is demonically inspired with themes of violence, immorality, and perversion. Most parents do not know what their children are listening to or don't know the danger posed by corrupt music. Satan was once involved in heaven's music. He uses it as a powerful medium of entry into many lives today.

The Demonization of a Believer
Chapter 6

This chapter is going to give some a pain that they can't locate.

One of the issues that I had to rethink when evil began to manifest itself was the possibility of the demonization of a believer. When asked if a Christian can be demonized, the stock answer is a resounding "no!". While that answer rests upon an assumption, I have not yet been able support it with direct scripture. In fact, I have found just the opposite to be true. I had attended three seminaries and had always been directed toward the principle that a Christian could not be demonized. All but one of the demonized people that I have dealt with were Christians. How could this be? The main argument has been that the Holy Spirit cannot coexist in the same body with a demon. But, in truth, He does share space with darkness in our continual dealings with sin.

A closer look into scripture revealed to me what I now embrace as truth. It is possible for a Christian to be demonized.

A Christian being possessed by a demon is not the question. Actually, the English translation of the word possessed doesn't give an accurate picture of the actual condition. The word used by the Holy Spirit in Greek (Matthew 4:24) is "daimonizomai" which accurately translates to be under the power or influence of a demon. It simply translates, directly, to be demonized. The word possessed tends to indicate total ownership and domination. There is no support for words like oppressed or possessed used in scripture. There is no distinction in the word to indicate other levels of control. Most of those who declare or insist that a Christian cannot be demonized base their belief on an assumption that finds no basis in scripture. It is a happy assumption but simply has no Biblical support. It should not be dared to build a theological case on Biblical matters without holding accurately to the language the Holy Spirit used to house the truths of the New Testament. To be influenced or controlled in some area of life is to be demonized.

In order to comprehend this, it is important to understand how humans are created. We are created very much like the Hebrew Temple. Our bodies have been referred to as the temple of the Holy Spirit (1 Corinthians 6:19).

There are three aspects of the Temple that mirror the human makeup. The **Outer Court** was the area where worshipers brought their sacrifices to be presented to God. This area was seen by all who assembled. Our body corresponds to this outer court. It is seen by all. It is world conscious.

The **Holy Place** was enclosed and housed the golden altar where incense was offered, the table of showbread, and the menorah. Only selected ones (priests) were allowed in this area. The Holy Place corresponds to our soul which houses our mind, will, and emotions. It is the buffer between our body (flesh) and our spirit. The Holy Place of mind, will, and emotions is self-conscious.

The third area of the temple was the **Holy of Holies**. It was where God's presence dwelt. Only the high priest could enter into the Holy of Holies one time a year to sprinkle blood for the atonement of the sins of the people. This, of course, relates to the human spirit. The human spirit is dead in trespasses and sin until the Holy Spirit brings life to it through His indwelling. This area is God conscious.

We are warned as believers not to "give place (topos) to the devil" (Ephesians 4:27). The Greek word topos indicates any space marked off from surrounding space. We are not to allow Satan a place in our place. A believer does not need to be completely controlled or dominated by a demonic spirit to be classified as demonized but rather only have a place in our life that comes under the influence or control of a demonic spirit.

Actually, the only safe deliverance is that of a believer. The gravity of driving out demonic spirits in an unsaved person as pictured in Matthew 12:43-45 is great. It can result in a terrible condition that possibly leads to a deeper bondage than was present in the original condition.

We find evidence of the Outer Court (body) being controlled by the demonic. In Luke 13:10-16, Jesus drives out a demon that had bound a Daughter of Abraham for eighteen years. Those standing near were physical Jews but Jesus did not refer to them as Sons of Abraham. Jesus later took somebody who was most likely not a physical Jew at all (Zacchaeus, who was an established resident of Jericho with a high ranking governmental position), and said very clearly that he was a child of Abraham because he believed upon Jesus (Luke 19:9). Romans 2:28-29 also makes it clear who a child of Abraham really is; "for he is not a Jew who is one outwardly, nor is circumcision that which is outward in the flesh. But he is a Jew who is one inwardly; and circumcision is that which is of the heart, by the Spirit, not by the letter; and his praise is not from men, but from God".

When one is troubled by the demonic in his physical body, it may manifest itself in many ways. Of course, sickness is a common manifestation although not all sickness comes from the demonic. The goal is the destruction of the body (kill, steal, destroy) and can ultimately lead to self-destruction through sin or suicide.

There are also examples of the Holy Place (soul) being under the influence of the demonic in that our mind, will, and emotions are beguiled or manipulated. James 3:14-15 warns believers of manifesting a mindset of demonic wisdom. 2 Corinthians 11:4 warns believers against receiving a different spirit than the one they had received. Paul indicated to

Timothy that in the latter times those of faith would fall away and follow after deceitful spirits and doctrines of demons (1 Timothy 4:1-2). A prime example of one's mind quickly becoming controlled by evil is Simon Peter and his great confession. In Matthew 16:16, Peter is proclaiming the truth that Jesus is the Christ, the Son of the living God. Only moments later, after an emotional outburst, Jesus calls Peter Satan himself and that he was a stumbling block to Him. When the Holy Spirit was moving in the early church, two married believers, Ananias and Sapphira, lied to the Holy Spirit and were rebuked as having allowed Satan to fill their hearts (Acts 5:3). A church member at Corinth was overcome by a spirit of lust and incest (1 Corinthians 5:5). Some in the Galatian church had been bewitched by others (Galatians 3:1).

When one is troubled by the demonic in his soul, the manifestations can be diverse and many. It is possible that even when an affliction like depression sets into someone that the demonic may take advantage of the malady and make it more severe. Not all of the following are completely demonically inspired but can be. Some manifestations may be unbelief, doubt, guilt, shame, confusion, schizophrenia, deceit, fear, resentment, bitterness, anger, rejection, and more.

The Holy of Holies (spirit) is where God dwells in one's life. It is only accessible by the High Priest (Jesus).

When one looks at the New Testament in light of demonization, it is clear that most of the cautions, warnings, and events dealing with the demonic involves believers.

The Believer's Authority
Chapter 7

When God gave Adam dominion over all of His creation (Genesis 1:26), Adam forfeited his authority by disobeying God and obeying the devil. There is no difference in saying no to God and saying yes to the devil. Either will cause us to give away our spiritual authority in life.

Since God has made provision for the recovery of spiritual authority by the blood of the cross, I am amazed at how many believers are living like P.O.W.'s when God has made it possible to live like Special Ops.

From Genesis 3 to Revelation 20, the Bible records constant conflict in the spirit world. The good news is that Satan has already been conquered at the cross and Jesus has made His authority available to every believer (Luke 10:19). Putting matters plainly, the Lord has made provision for our being overcomers.

The only way a believer can fail in spiritual warfare is to refuse to fight. I am constantly amazed at the number of Christians who simply do not even try to resist Satan much less battle with him.

They make it so easy for the devil. They seem intimidated by him or they are simply too lazy to learn the enemy and principles of defeating him in their life. Satan is not the evil counterpart of God. He is no god at all. He is a created being and can certainly be overcome by the authority of an everlasting God.

What is the meaning of this spiritual authority given to follows of Jesus? It means that the One who has the ultimate authority (Matthew 28:18) has offered the use of that authority to all who, by faith, will embrace and stand in it.

The authority that I have is a delegated power from a higher source, it does not come naturally to me but rather supernaturally. This authority allows me to take spiritual control over my mind, home, finances, and practically every area of my life in order to bring glory to God. What areas of your life are out of control? We have the authority to control these areas by the power of His might.

The authority offered to me is representative in nature. I must never think that this authority originates or finds its power in my own heart.

I have always been amazed that a 160-pound man with a uniform can hold out his hand and stop and 3-ton vehicle. It is not the policeman's personal authority that makes the truck stop but rather what his uniform represents. A large truck could easily ignore his signals and pass right over him but will not because of where the policeman's authority rests.

When I was in grade school there were occasions when the teacher needed to leave the classroom and we students were left alone. There was no chaos in the teacher's absence because she always left a student in charge of "taking names" of anyone who acted out of line. The one in my room most often chosen to be the name taker was a boy named Brad. Brad was a nerd before nerdism became fashionable. There was not a boy in our class, nor several girls, who couldn't easily stand up against Brad but never did because of the teacher's authority given to him. It was as though the teacher never left the room with Brad acting in her authority.

I must never reach the point of spiritual arrogance to believe that I have any power over the devil. I rest in the fact that Jesus has given me His power to stand against the enemy. I represent the Savior King in my day to day dealings with Satan.

The purpose of the authority of the Lord Jesus is multiple in nature. Primarily, it allows me to live successfully in enemy territory. Isaiah 25:7 reveals that the earth is enveloped in a canopy of darkness. Satan is atmospheric, being the "prince of the power of the air" (Ephesians 2:2). This veil of darkness is spread over all nations so that no one alive can live outside of its influence. Perhaps this is why Jesus comes back to take His raptured saints out of the world by meeting us in the air as typified in Revelation 4:1. He opens a door through this darkness to transport His children of light. <u>The war is real in this fallen world. Peace is a marker of the absence of war. In those areas of life where there is no peace, there is war.</u> I have the authority in Christ to extend God's peace to the areas of my life where war is raging. Jesus has the ability to extend peace even to a storm threatening to sink His boat.

When I was a child, we played a game called "King of the Hill". The purpose was to place oneself at the top of a pile of dirt or small hill and fend off every challenger trying to remove you and take your place as king of the hill. When one larger than other challengers was at the top, it was virtually impossible to remove him. Satan has set himself up in this world as king of the hill but Jesus made an open fool of him through the cross (Colossians 2:15) and extends that same power to me in removing Satan as king of the hill that my life sets upon.

Another purpose of His offered authority is to allow the believer to live in victory over the adversity that sin and the devil causes. There are approximately 328 New Testament references to supernatural evil operating around us at all times. In my experience with those who are battling demonization, I have identified four levels of demonic activity attempting to ensnare one in its grasp.

It begins as **influence**, progresses to **afflictions**, then gives over to **bondage** and finally results in **dominion**. In order to resist and overcome these forces, there must be power strong enough to resist these successfully. Is it possible for a Christian to control adversity in his life? It is possible to control adversity to the point that God allows in the power of His authority. Matthew 16:19 gives us authority to bind and release in His name.

A close look at the language the Holy Spirit used in revealing this to Matthew clears up some passed-on ignorance about this passage. A deeper look into the wording will reveal that "whatever you bind on earth will have **already** been bound in heaven and whatever you loose on earth will have **already** been loosed in heaven." I don't dictate to God what I want bound or loosed, I simply follow on earth what He has **already** established in heaven. As Satan (and his demons) look for a body to put their power and control on, so does the Holy Spirit look for one who is willing to stand against the darkness to release light and peace. Satan is described as a roaring lion seeking whom he may devour (1 Peter 5:8) but as in Daniel's situation, we know that God has no trouble controlling lions. Neither should we.

It is clear that God expects the redeemed to live as overcomers (to him who overcomes I will give …) and to be more than conquerors. The only way to attain that level of living is to embrace and live in His authority while living in the kingdom of darkness. How can one be more than a conqueror (Romans 8:37)? Where a conqueror falls short is in two areas. Even though he expands his reach by being a conqueror, eventually another, stronger conqueror will rise up to take his kingdom and he will lose his possessions gained by successful warfare. A believer need never lose what he has taken in the Lord's name. Thus, more than a conqueror. Many times, a conqueror must stand alone at the top when perils and threats come. The believer is never alone because he is never at the top. There is always one greater than the Christian and he never needs to feel alone in times of peril. Thus, more than a conqueror. This provides a life of never ending joy and peace.

How does one move into a position of spiritual authority? <u>The journey into spiritual victory begins with learning how to resist the devil (James 4:7) so that he will flee. He must be resisted instantly, continuously, boldly, unitedly if possible, and with the aid of tried armor (Ephesians 6). My duty begins with drawing near to God since I will be resisting in His power</u>. There comes a point when I must say no to Satan and stand strong. I don't have to take what he dishes out. I don't have to sit back in despair and watch him destroy my children or marriage.

When I was a child we used a phrase toward our siblings or friends that said, "I don't have to do what you say because you're not the boss of me." I now have the ability to say the same to the devil. He no longer is the boss of me, Jesus is my Lord.

I must also establish a spiritual self-worth. Many establish a self-worth based on what people say about them. It is fragile at best and mostly inaccurate. A spiritual self-worth is built by believing what God says about a believer. It includes forgiveness, grace, value, etc. While I may not feel worthy to represent His name, He has made me worthy by the blood and sees me as an overcomer when I don't see this in myself. So, by faith, I embrace the value that He places on me and I embrace the authority that He offers. I am not worthy to carry the authority of His name but the Jesus in me is.

With these factors in place, I am now ready to take control of my life before God and accomplish His purpose. This begins with the name of Jesus on my lips and is consummated with the likeness of Jesus in my heart. Once I set my heart toward the Lord in faith, then I will receive His authority, wait for Satan to test it, and stand firm by faith in the battle. The believer will never stand stronger than with a working knowledge of the Word of God and the ability to say to the devil "<u>it is written …</u>".

This authority is especially needed by fathers. As the strong man of the home, it is your responsibility to stand in protection over your family. We once had a teenage girl who was active in the church's youth activities and was a normal teen in many ways but began to manifest demonically at youth camp one summer. Our youth pastor tried dealing with it but couldn't bring her to a point of deliverance. He called me and asked what to do. Knowing that her father was a strong believer, I told him to call her father to come to the camp. He called and the father said he would be there as quickly as he could. When the youth pastor told the manifesting spirit (a sultry, sexual spirit) that her father was on the way, the spirit left her immediately and she never had another problem with the demonic realm again. <u>Spiritually wimpy fathers watch their families fall apart and only gripe about it. Spirit filled fathers are able to do the battle for their family when necessary.</u>

When our son turned 15, we were in one of the greatest growth and revival times of our church's history. I was the senior pastor when I learned that our son was involved in drugs and alcohol. We acted immediately by putting him rehab and starting the process of helping him to correct the behavior. We were not encouraged when the counselors told us that there was only a ten percent success rate among teenagers in rehab. At first this was discouraging. After many weeks, it seemed as though there was no progress being made. This drove me to a point of antagonism toward the enemy. I refused to let him have my son. I began fasting before the Lord and praying in warfare mode to salvage my son's life. On the fourth day of the fast, God gave me a promise from His word in Isaiah 60:4, "You son shall come from afar, and your daughter shall be nursed at your side." I quickly embraced this promise by faith and stood on it. Within a couple of days, the battle was over. After many weeks of no progress, there was a complete turn around and my son was released from the bondage and returned to the unity of the home and our daughter never left our side until she married. Our son is now a pastor and our daughter is married to a pastor. <u>I refuse to let Satan take my family or anything else God has blessed me with. I don't have to since He gave me His authority to deal with the enemy</u>.

When Jesus Confronts the Enemy
Chapter 8

Jared was a teenager who had begun to manifest demonic behavior at certain times. When I sat down to talk with Jared, I learned that a close family member, a male, had begun a homosexual relationship with him when he was only a child. Now, the enemy had a resident power that controlled Jared often. I began the intervention.

"Tell me your name." I said.

"Go away, I don't have anything to do with you," the spirit said.

"I am your conqueror in Christ Jesus." I reaffirmed.

"You have no power over me, you are a sinner just like me," this spirit said.

"Yes, but my sins have been washed away by the blood of Jesus," I reminded him.

"I own this boy, he gave himself to me," he said.

"But it was not his to give. He is bought with a price, the blood of Jesus," I said.

"I won't leave," he said.

"You will leave and you will leave now. You will take every other spirit with you."

"Why should I?" he asked.

"I am acting in the authority of Jesus Christ who holds all power over you. It is His will that you go. So, leave now," I demanded.

He left.

The first confrontation recorded between Satan and Jesus while He was on the earth is in Matthew 4:1. The Holy Spirit set up the bout in the wilderness for Satan to attempt to tempt the Lord. Of course, we know that Satan got nowhere in his efforts. Early in the ministry of Jesus Satan tried to distract Him and derail Him in His mission. There was a reason why this was important to His enemy.

When Jesus entered the world as a human, He came to make a difference, to change things. There is no parallel event in the Old Testament that had as much impact as it did when God became a man. Jesus brought Kingdom power with Him and established that power and authority in the hearts of those who believed in Him. If we think Satan has great power today, how much more did he have before Jesus came with His authority and power?

Jesus announced that the Kingdom has come (Matthew 10:7). The evidence of the Kingdom of heaven being near was twofold: proclamation and demonstration. This is revealed in Isaiah 61:1-3 and in Luke 4:18-21. He sent His disciples out in demonstration of His power in Matthew 10:1. They cast out demons and healed the sick. There is no evidence that God had ever before given such power to multiple people at one time as He did the disciples. Jesus proclaimed (Luke 11:20) that if He cast out demons by the finger of God, that was an indication that the Kingdom of God had come. Matthew 12:28 identifies the finger of God as the Holy Spirit who also created the heavens (Psalm 8:3), wrote the ten commandments (Exodus 31:18), and showed His power before Pharaoh in Egypt (8:19). Not only did He begin to do great damage against the kingdom of Satan but He expects us to do the same in His name (John 14:12) because as the Father has sent Him, He sends us (John 20:21). There would be five generations of Kingdom developments to establish God's authority in the earth and leave a permanent presence until the end. Of course, it began with **Jesus,** who is God, stepping into time and space. He then commissioned the **disciples** to do His work. From the work they were doing, He established the **church** and gave it life and power at Pentecost. He then sent out **proclaimers** such as Paul, Peter, and others to extend the reach of the church. Once the church was established, He called **leaders** and installed apostles, prophets, evangelists, and pastor teachers (Ephesians 4:11) to give guidance to the church. This ensured that His body would be fixed upon the earth right in the center of the kingdom of darkness.

Satan's defeat began in the wilderness encounter with Jesus of Matthew 4:1. Jesus walked onto Satan's turf unafraid and without hesitation. Satan tempted Him on the same basis that he tempted Adam and Eve. He tested and tempted in relation to obedience to God. What he apparently did not know is that Jesus could not sin. Sin was not even in the realm of possibility for Jesus. We sin because we have a sin nature. We are not sinners because we sin, we sin because we are sinners. Jesus had no sin nature so it was never in Him to sin.

Titus 1:2 states that God cannot lie. Not that He won't lie, but that He cannot lie. It isn't in Him to do so. James 1:13 declares that God cannot be tempted because temptation appeals to a fallen and sinful nature that Jesus did not possess. His nature is impeccable. This is why we need His life in us in order to overcome temptation and sin.

Satan's strategy is not difficult to identify. He seeks to prevent God from being glorified by keeping lost people from being saved and saved people in bondage. 2 Corinthians 4:4 reveals that the god of this world has blinded the minds of those who do not believe lest the light of the gospel of the glory of Christ should shine on them. When that statement is placed next to 2 Timothy 2:4 proclaiming that God desires all men to be saved and to come to the knowledge of truth, it is not difficult to discern the enemy's strategy. In so doing, he desires to make people and cultures as miserable as possible in life with his steal, kill, and destroy intentions (John 10:10). Saved people have a choice in this. The saved have something to say about this strategy and are not subject to the devil's plans unless it is by choice or surrender.

In light of Satan's defeat at the cross, the Holy Spirit carries the authority of Jesus to us thereby giving us the power to pull down strongholds that the enemy has established (2 Corinthians 10:4-5). Jesus has brought the war to Satan on his own turf. He is effectively doing battle now through those who stand in His authority.

We use His power over strongholds through "**truth encounters**" (casting down arguments), "**allegiance encounters**" (every thought into captivity to the obedience of Christ), and through "**power encounters**" (every high thing that exalts itself against the knowledge of God). God has chosen His people, even called them (1 Corinthians 1:26) to nullify the things that are (1 Corinthians 1:28).

This is demonstrated in Daniel's praying through in spite of territorial spirits (Daniel 10). Jeremiah had authority to pull down powers over entire cities and nations (Jeremiah 1:10). Paul opened an entire continent in power in the face of much opposition (Acts 19:10, 20).

When Satan confronted Jesus with the absurd idea that Jesus would surrender in worship to him, he had no idea that his kingdom of darkness was about to be invaded with much success by the One who had the authority to do so.

Confronting the Enemy
Chapter 9

It is a defining moment when a Christian comes to accept his authority in Jesus Christ and has the ability to change things that stand against the will of God in his life. <u>There is no greater surge of spiritual energy than that which happens when the believer, standing in the authority of Jesus, sees the enemy defeated in some area of life.</u>

The battle began in the heavens. The scripture identifies three heavens. The first heaven is where the birds fly and the clouds drift. We are surrounded by this firmament while living our lives. The second heaven declares the glory of God through the stars, planets, and other bodies in space. The third heaven is where God dwells. Paul said that he was caught up into the third heaven and disallowed to speak of what he saw.

Sin originated in the third heaven. When Satan was banished from the dwelling place of God, he came to make the earth his base of operation, thus taking control of the first heaven and placing a canopy of evil around it (Isaiah 25:7). He filled it with superstition, idolatry, ignorance, and deception. Ephesians 2:2 calls him the prince of the power of the air and he is always busy.

At this point, God had a dilemma. The first dilemma was the question of how can a pure and holy God come to a people who are following hard after sin and Satan? Before the death, burial, and resurrection of Jesus, Satan had the authority to govern the creation that Adam had been given dominion over. Within the creation, under the veil of darkness, he created a cosmic graveyard where all who were in his realm were dead in trespasses and sin (Ephesians 2:1). Everyone outside of the grace that Jesus made possible were dead and buried under the broken nature of their sin. These were hopelessly destined to follow the course of death.

The second dilemma, related to the first, was how can God rescue these dead ones from this graveyard of sin when it is legally controlled by another? God had answers for both questions. He establishes a new presence and authority in the usurped heavenly places. Ephesians 1:3 reveals that the Father God inserted spiritual blessings into the realm of Satan's realm. He also placed the resurrected Jesus to rule higher than any other authority over the heavenly places (Ephesians 1:20-21). He then positioned the church to be planted in these heavenly places (Ephesians 2:6). He uses the church to instruct the principalities and powers in heavenly places of His work and will (Ephesians 3:10). He has equipped believers with the proper armor to take the fight to the rulers of darkness (Ephesians 6:10-12). This battle is against four levels of demonic regimentation: **Principalities** (powerful territorial spirits), **powers** (more numerous and less independent than principalities), **rulers of darkness** (responsibilities on local levels to propagate sin and darkness), and **spiritual wickedness** – or directly translated – spiritual powers of evil - (numerous spirits who function like worker bees. There was a whole legion of these dwelling in one man - Mark 5:9). Evil used in this passage is the word we get our word pornography from. Their work is one of depravity and perversion. These are the forces that God set His people against with enough authority to be successful in the battle.

God's strategy to infiltrate Satan's territory is revealed in Ephesians as follows: He will seed the heavenly places with blessings (1:3) like seeds under snow. He will place Jesus in the lowest (grave) and highest places (exaltation) on Satan's turf

(1:20-21). He then will place His church in the middle of this kingdom of darkness (2:6). He will reveal His truth and will to the enemy through His body the church (3:10). Finally, He will confront the high powers through His people who have been made strong in the power of His might (6:10-12).

In this plan, God has established some constants, things that are not negotiable. Jesus' position of authority as the head and feet will always be true. Grace will allow our holy God to move sinners from Satan's graveyard of sin into heavenly places. The church now is potentially in control of the heavenly places as Satan was defeated at the cross. The church, under Jesus' authority, is God's liberating army. The only variable in this equation is what the church decides to do or not do.

In order for believers to establish spiritual dominion in the earth, they must be wise and powerful in their strategy. Here are the steps in bringing down the keepers of darkness. These principles not only enable the church to be victorious, but also work in the individual believer's life to conquer the spiritual threats in their dominions.

The first step is to identify Satan's legal grounds of residence in an area. Ephesians 4:27 demands that we give no grounds to the devil. The word used here in Greek is "Topos" which is a region, an area. Satan will not challenge Jesus' authority directly but feels free to challenge God through the believer's life. Eden is an example of an indirect attack on God through Eve. So, the individual or collection of saints must be ready to do battle with him. The church or believer's spiritual strength will determine how strong the influence of darkness is.

In looking at the USA regionally, the Northeast is dominated by liberal moral standards while the West is dominated by secularism or cults. The South continues to have a spirit of religion rather than raw spirituality. Through spiritual mapping, it can be determined how these spiritual conditions came to be. Those conditions, based upon Satan's lies, must be countered by truth which will set individuals and regions free. In times of national revivals, when truth has been spread and embraced, whole regions were reclaimed for the gospel. It must be determined when and how the grounds were given over to darkness.

Once the enemy is identified and his reasons for legal ownership is established, the battle begins. Remember, there is only one enemy. People are not the enemy of the Kingdom of God, their master is. This is when the body of Christ begins to exercise their authority in Christ. Satan's fear, like Pharaoh in Exodus 1:10, is that the church, the collection of saints will embrace the authority that God offers to them as revealed in 1 John 4:4. The battle will be based upon powerful warfare praying. The reason the church seems powerless today to stop the drift into deeper darkness is because our prayers seem to be written by lawyers or writers who provide God a way out in the case that no answer comes. We excuse the lack of response of God to prayer by saying that God answers in three ways. He says yes, no, or wait awhile. That philosophy did not come from the Bible. **We have developed a theology of powerlessness.**

Once God is involved by prayer (the only way to get God involved in anything) then the actions of believers will be to state and declare the truth in order to displace lies as Jesus did in Matthew 4:4, 7, 10. The word of God should be used against Satan. The believer should demand, in the authority of Jesus, that he release the ground he holds and leave (Matthew 4:10; James 4:7). If necessary, believers should unite in evicting him (Romans 15:30. Begin with prayer then stand on truth. Win the battle in the air first through prayer then, send in the ground troops.)

The powerful church should begin seeing captives set free (Acts 26:18). The believers will be able to plunder the strong man's house (Matthew 12:29) and release back to God what the devil has stolen. The will of God will be loosed (Matthew 16:19) in the area once dominated by the will of Satan.

The truth about ownership has been established. The creation belongs to God both by creation and redemption. The heavens declare His glory (Psalm 24:1). The people of Jesus' name will bind the powers of darkness with worship and truth (Psalm 149:5-9) because it is the Father's good pleasure to give His people the Kingdom (Luke 12:32).

Prayer is Warfare
Chapter 10

I once stopped by a church building that had meant much to me in my younger years. The church was without a pastor and had other needs. I asked for a key to the sanctuary so that I could go inside and pray for the church.

Once inside, I turned on a single light over the pulpit/altar area. I knelt by the altar and began praying. The church had been plagued by sin through the years in the some of the former leadership and I was praying against that stronghold in this church. As I prayed, the light over me clicked off. I arose, went to the light switch to find it turned off. I flipped it back on then went back to my prayer place. The light clicked off again. I turned it on again. This went on several times until I simply ignored the distracting light and continued to pray. I knew that the enemy was trying to keep me from praying the authority of Jesus over this church. These demonic spirits are sometimes like bad children that cannot harm, only cause trouble.

~~The only way to get God involved in the events of my life is through prayer.~~ We are not attempting to get a fix from God through prayer, but rather we are trying to get God fixed in a matter by prayer. Warfare praying happens in different levels of intensity. Sometimes we can pray through to victory in mere moments, sometimes hours, sometimes days, and many times with fasting. I have known some to pray in faith for years before breaking through to the desired goal. It is my conviction that most Christians pray for too many things at a time (long prayer lists), not being able to focus on a single major issue. Which is better, to pray over thirty-seven matters at a time without focus and nothing being answered or over one major need that we can focus our faith on and see it come to pass? Many pray often but without the depth and faith needed to change things in the spirit world. I may not always be in a war but when I am, prayer is my greatest weapon against the enemy.

We are given a strong lesson on warfare praying in Luke 18:1-8. There are two important attitudes in prayer that are necessary to win our battles according to verse one. We must pray **constantly**. We are instructed to pray without giving up. Some translations use the words "to faint" or to "lose heart". The truth is we must never stop praying until something is resolved. We are to pray until the answer comes. Some would call this prevailing in prayer or praying through. The promise to stand on is Jeremiah 33:3. If we call, God said He would answer. "I will answer" is the assurance that we have in Him. Never give up. Never stop. Never quit. How long should we pray over a matter? Always!!

We also learn a second attitude in our praying from this passage. We are to pray **aggressively**. We are the overcomers, conquerors, and victors. We are not praying toward victory, we are praying from victory, the cross. Those who pray passively are in bondage to praying with wishing and hoping. Even if some could be bold in prayer, too many cancel their bold praying by tacking on "If it be your will" at the end of it. That allows us to save face if God does not answer. If we are embracing His promises when we pray, we know what His will is and must pray in that authority. It is better to seek God's will about a matter for days and pray in light of that will for only a few moments than to pray for days not knowing what God's will is, thus not being able to pray in faith. Remember, faith comes from the Word of God (Romans 10:17). Study long about God's will and pray strong rather than praying long without knowing what God wants. The believer's aggressive prayer frees him to pray in faith with freedom to believe in the face of discouraging events. <u>Don't depend on others' prayers, learn to pray powerfully yourself along with inviting others to agree with you (Matthew 18:19) in a matter before God.</u>

To pray in authority based upon God's will sets captives free. I was once involved in a worship service where God was doing some significant work. There was a lot of brokenness and repentance among those present. The altars were full and people were being set free. I stood among those praying at the altars helping people. A teenager named Will walked over to me with big tears in his eyes. I asked how I could help him. He told me that his heart was broken over his lost friend Timmy. Timmy was present that night in the service but was unmoved by the Holy Spirit as so many others were. I asked Will what he thought God's will was for Timmy concerning salvation. He said he believed that Jesus wanted to save him. I said how do you know that? He quoted 1 Timothy 2:4 to me. He believed that "God our Savior wants all people to be saved and to come to a knowledge of the truth". I asked Will if he believed that the Lord would save Timmy if we agreed in prayer about God 's will in the matter. He looked deep into my eyes and after a moment of consideration, said with a strong confidence, "Yes!" I knew at that moment that the Holy Spirit had just filled his heart with faith based on what the Bible said. I prayed with Will about Timmy's salvation, asking God to work quickly in Timmy's life and change his heart. We both wept before the Lord as we prayed. When we had finished praying, Will turned to go back to his seat and ran smack into to Timmy who was standing immediately behind him waiting to talk to me. Will hugged Timmy's neck without saying anything to him and left him standing there. I asked Timmy how I could help him. He said, in brokenness, that he wanted to be saved. He called on the Lord in faith and repentance and the Lord saved him on the spot. Never again would Will pray passively. He had seen God do an amazing work quickly, right before his eyes.

To pray effectively for the lost is to first understand their condition. That condition is detailed in 2 Corinthians 4:3-4. The gospel is hidden from them by having their eyes blinded by the enemy. To pray effectively for them, the blinders must be

<u>torn off so that the glorious light of the gospel will penetrate their soul, bringing them to salvation.</u> This is done through warfare praying.

In Luke 18, Jesus gives us a powerful picture of prayer. Seemingly, the worst judge that could be had is the one pictured in the story. This judge is independent. He stood alone in his actions. He was not influenced by man or God. He made his own decisions. Let's use the characters in the story Jesus told to get an application for our praying. Let's let God be portrayed by this judge. He makes His own decisions without counsel from anyone. Satan has our loved one in bondage and we are going to take him before the judge whose name is on the docket. We are going before God on behalf of the one held in bondage. In order to build a case against the enemy, I am going to look through the list of attorneys available and find one to represent me who has the same last name as the judge.

Scripture says that there is one mediator, He is Jesus (1 Timothy 2:5). Now, I have Jesus as the One to represent me before His Father, the judge. When can we go before the judge? Right now! I walk into the courtroom together with my attorney, the son of the Judge and boldly tell the Judge of my need. Satan is helpless at this point. He stands outside of the will of the Judge and cannot influence the case against the intercession of my attorney, Jesus. The Judge then rules in favor of His Son.

There is in this story, told by Jesus, an exciting promise to those who pray. Verse eight promises that the Judge will avenge us in our cause. God has taken it upon Himself to make the wrong right. I will gladly let Him do what He is determined to do. Once I know what the Judge is determined to do, I am going to stand back and watch Him work. It is indicated that He has the authority to avenge our cause speedily. Verse seven declares that He does this for the "elect". Who are the elect? All the "whosoever wills" that belong to Him.

How long does it take God to answer my prayer? Speedily! If there is no speedy answer, I don't ask what is wrong with God, but rather what is wrong with me? If there is something between me and the Father, I must clear that up before I can expect Him to answer (Psalm 66:18). God is looking for faith. Faith comes from believing what God says, not what I want to be true. Too many pray and then just shrug when there is no answer. The battle is real and the answer very often requires doing the warfare.

Psalm 149:6 gives us another weapon for our prayer battle. We are to do warfare with the high praises of God in our mouth. When we pray, we attack. When I am filled with His Spirit (Ephesians 5:18), the high praises of God flow out of my heart. The high praises of God is God's Spirit in me praising God in heaven. When we are filled with His Spirit, we trade places with God in our inner man. Then, as His Spirit is praising within me, I pray until the release that He has heard me comes. I pray until He has assured me about the answer. What happens in worship? Praise and faith mingle together. God is exalted and Satan is defeated. The will of God becomes the law of the heart and cancels the enemy's work. Vengeance is accomplished (Luke 18:7) and the adversary is defeated (Luke 18:8). God's praise in our mouth and God's Word in our heart brings aggressive action against the kingdom of darkness.

Prayer is Binding Satan
Chapter 11

How does God get into a matter? By prayer.

How is a Christian to deal with the devil? By prayer.

How often should one pray? Constantly.

How long should one pray? Until the answer comes.

Remember we won.

Where did we win? At the cross.

How did we win? By the blood.

Of Whom? Jesus Christ, the Son of God.

Spiritual warfare can be described as gaining deliverance through prayer. In Matthew 6:13, as Jesus was teaching us to pray, He said that we were to pray for deliverance from the evil one. 2 Corinthians 4:4 calls Satan the god of this world which means that we live on his turf and he never gives up trying to block the will of God on earth.

A quick look around confirms that Satan is having his way for the most part. There are millions of witches in the U.S.A. A great majority of teens are unchurched. Addictions, perversions, and darkness are on the rise. There is a growing membership in the Satanic Church. Satanists practice their arts within easy distance of most churches without any repercussions in the spirit world.

It is the purpose of prayer to establish the will of God on the earth as it is in heaven (Matthew 6:10) and it is expected by God that believers will fight for that. This is a much different perspective than religion gives. Religion tries to get God to join its plans. Victorious believers find out what God is doing and join Him in it. It must be remembered that everyday of our lives are laid out before we ever live the first one (Psalm 139:16). God has directed our life to be lived within His will that was established for before we were born (Ephesians 2:10). It is Satan's strategy to attempt to interrupt our living up to what God has written about us in His book.

How did Jesus do the will of God? He first established that the will of the Father was the only thing He was sent to do on the earth. He stepped into Satan's domain to cut across the enemy's desires and establish the will of God in the earth. John 5:17, 19, and 30 states that God is always at work and Jesus was busy doing what the Father desired. The work Jesus did was not His own but rather the will of God. Every work, every miracle, every word was God's, not His. He established God's will in every matter.

The work of the devil is to kill, steal, and destroy. He has been doing this since the beginning (John 10:10) and it is the purpose of Jesus to destroy the enemy's work (1John 3:8). Because of the threat posed by Jesus, Satan was threatened by the Lord all the way back to Bethlehem. Even then, Satan attempted to block the Savior's way. The strategy of Satan is to weaken the church through division (Matthew 12:25) simply because the church is the body of light in the devil's domain. He does this by sowing discord and division among church people.

Several years ago, a talk show hosted a self-proclaimed Satanist and questioned the strategy of weakening the work of believers in the world. His plan was to join a church with the intention of being contentious in order to cause such division among its members that the church becomes spiritually ineffective. When a church stops praying because of strife and division, Satan has won. The church is then spiritually impotent. The first ones to follow such division and stand against raw spirituality of being Spirit led, are the professional religionists (Matthew 12:22-24). This is the reason why God hates any who sow discord among believers in the church (Proverbs 6:16-19).

So, how is the church to do warfare against the spiritual wickedness in their area? According to Matthew 12:29, we are to bind the strong man, this is the will of God. Since Satan is not omnipresent (can't be multiple places at one time), we find ourselves not binding Satan as a being, but rather his workers, the demon spirits that keep his kingdom operating. After the strong man is bound, we are to plunder his house. 2 Corinthians 4:4 indicates that this includes setting the spiritually blind and captives free. We are to release, in Jesus' name, that which rightly belongs to God by creation and redemption. We are to release what Satan has stolen.

How does one bind the strong man and plunder his house? It is the finger of God that accomplishes this action. We are to point the finger of God at the work of the devil. The finger of God first appears in Egypt (Exodus 8:19) when by God's power the dust became gnats. The magicians of Egypt could not reproduce this miracle. We are also told that the finger of God inscribed the stone tablets given to Moses on the mountain (Exodus 31:18). When Jesus was dealing with the demonic forces of His day, He cast out demons by the finger of God (Luke 11:19-20) and Matthew identifies the finger of God as the Spirit of God (Matthew 12:27-28).

Christians go to God in prayer, in the name of Jesus, based upon the will of God to cast out the darkness and set captives free. This prayer becomes mighty through God (2 Corinthians 10:4) and pulls down strongholds of the enemy. The finger of God (Holy Spirit) is activated and dispatched against the enemy and applies the power of the blood to overcome Satan's minions. Satan's forces are bound by the power of the blood (Revelation 12:10). This blood was the means of his defeat at the cross. The captives are then released.

Those matters that are spiritually established, the things that presently are, must be torn down.

In 1 Corinthians 1:26-28, God has chosen and called the believer to nullify (bring to nothing) the things that are. It begins with faith that Jesus has given us His power to trample over the enemy (Luke 10:19). We invoke by faith the powerful name of Jesus, pray the prayer of faith, apply the blood of Jesus, and command that the captives be released.

Prayer is the main weapon in the arsenal of a believer. Nothing, no situation, person, or event lies outside of the reach of prayer. What God does for the believer, He does because of prayer. We have not because we ask not.

Dealing With Strongholds
Chapter 12

Angie was a regular visitor in our worship services. She slipped in quietly and didn't remain when the service was over. I knew that she was seeking but not sure where she was spiritually. She avoided conversation with me and only knew a few people in our congregation. Then, God blew through our church in a strong move of His Spirit. There was a lot of repentance and life change in the weeks to follow as the Holy Spirit continued a tremendous work of revival. The details of this move of God are recorded in my book, **Walking In The Wind**. Angie was broken in this move of God and in her brokenness found her way back to Him. She wrote me letter detailing her journey. She had married and had a child. She began to participate in pornography with her husband. She had become a Christian as a young woman but this sin began to draw her away spiritually until finally she walked away from her fellowship with the Lord. But now, she was back and in the years to follow became a strong, renewed believer with no debris from her former sin. She continues on today strong in the Lord as does her grown child. She had recovered ground that she had surrendered to the enemy in her younger years and the stronghold was broken.

Satan has a clear strategy for a Christian's defeat. There are several weapons in his arsenal which can be used in accomplishing this.

Sin is his beginning work. It is a powerful weapon against us. He attempts to use our broken nature of sin to lure us into areas of defeat. If he can keep us in sin, then our sure failure happens because we are cut off from heartfelt and faith filled praying (Psalm 66:18). Prayer is our greatest weapon of both defense and offense in spiritual warfare. Our fellowship with God is broken by continual sin and thus, cuts us off from the powerful presence and work of the Holy Spirit. Sin seeks one like a missile. When it hits, it is immediately known simply because the Holy Spirit points it out. Actually, sin is one of the easiest forces to recover from. It is simply repentance and forsaking the sin that is besetting to us.

Another weapon in his arsenal is a passive work of **accusation**. Revelation 12:10 names Satan as the accuser. In fact, his very name means "slanderer". He stood before God and accused Job. If he has the courage to stand before God to accuse, imagine what he will say to me. He will remind us of every sin we have committed, the shame we should carry, and the unfit condition of our heart to call ourselves people of God. He attempts to convince us of our uselessness to God. According to Satan, we are too bad to be blessed.

Satan not only accuses us, he accuses God to us. He would have us convinced that God is doing a poor job managing our life because of what He allows to happen to us. Satan screams at us about God forsaking us and ignoring our prayers and cries for help. At this point, there is a real chance that fear could replace faith in my heart and despair will drive out hope. This attack can be dispelled by rejecting Satan's lies and embracing the truth. In order to be successful in this, we must have a working knowledge of the Bible which contains the truths we need to embrace.

Strongholds is one of the most lasting weapons that Satan will use against us. The power of a stronghold settles into an area of life where we suffer regular defeat. A stronghold can also be established by willingly giving an area of life over to sin on a regular basis. It is then an area of life where sin has entrenched itself. At this point, we no longer control the sin but rather sin controls us. This sin now becomes a besetting sin (Hebrews 12:1). An appetite has been developed for a particular sin of the flesh, mind, or heart and now has roots. It is through this stronghold that Satan manipulates us into constant defeat and the spiritual discouragement that accompanies it. We now find ourselves in bondage to sin. He has taken control of our life by establishing a stronghold.

I have known those who have developed a stronghold of addiction, hatred, violence, anger, gossip and other deviations away from the Spirit-filled life.

I once spoke to a young man with elementary aged children who explained away his attitude toward a particular behavior by blaming it on his father. He said that his father felt this way, he himself feels this way, and his children will feel this way. This had now become a generational stronghold that spanned at least three generations. We will deal with generational sin later in this book.

John was a preacher who spoke to me once revealing that he was bothered by the demonic. I asked how the spirit manifested in him and said through sexual perversions, pornography, and lust. I began to deal with the spirit that was controlling him. When the demonic spirit was forced to reveal himself, he called himself Romulon. He was very strong and had been in place for a very long time. I asked John about the door that this spirit felt free to enter his life by. He stated that he first knew something was controlling areas of his life when he was eight years old. He revealed to me that he had later become a teenage male prostitute for homosexuals. Even after many experiences with God and a fair success in ministry, he could not overcome this stronghold in his life that this sin had established. In our dealing with the spirits that bothered him, Romulon and eleven other demonic spirits like him were removed from his life and those strongholds were released although he still had to deal with the appetites he had developed for these sins but that was much easier to control than the stronghold had been.

A stronghold is an active, working spiritual fortress in our life. It is like a powerful force that has set up headquarters in an area of our life.

The power of a stronghold is secrecy. Without confession and repentance, and sometimes accountability, the stronghold will never be torn down. Its purpose is to control and ensure spiritual defeat. A stronghold stands on certain lies that we embrace as truth. It is a mental attitude with spiritual consequences.

Someone once said that a stronghold is a mindset filled with hopelessness that causes one to accept as unchangeable, situations we know to be contrary to the will of God in our life. It is defeating in its power to control to the point that many give up trying to overcome it and so condition their life to accommodate it. At this point, we clearly know God's will about this matter but reality is a different story. We find ourselves powerless to change a situation that is clearly a contradiction of God.

A stronghold acts to create double mindedness in us. This affects all that we do. James 1:8 declares that a double minded person is unstable in all of his ways and should not expect his prayers to be answered. A stronghold exposes a severe contradiction in what we say we are and what we really are. The visible expression of a stronghold is inconsistency. It tends to manifest itself in one who knows what God wills but has absolutely no power over it. He finds it impossible to do God's will in the matter. It allows us to compartmentalize areas of our lives to accommodate God's will in one area and to have the works of the mind or flesh active in another area. A stronghold must be destroyed in order to have consistency before God in our day to day walk.

Strongholds can be based in the **heart** with racial prejudice, resentment or bitterness, narcissism, etc. They also can take root in the **mind** with fear, gossip, confusion, depression, etc. Of course, there is a large susceptibility to strongholds with our **flesh** in compulsive or addictive behaviors. No matter where they find a place for their roots, they must be torn down.

2 Corinthians 10:3-5 details for the believer how to bring down a stronghold. It is important to be reminded at this point that this passage is written to the collection of saints called the church, not lost people. The word in Greek that the Holy Spirit used in verse 4 is the word "ochuroma". It is the only time this word is used in the New Testament. It is a word that is used to

describe a castle or fortress. In the case of spiritual strongholds, it is built on arguments and reasonings by which one endeavors to fortify his position and to defend against his opponent. In other words, it will be a fight in order to tear it down. The destruction of a stronghold requires three different types of encounters. The first is a **truth encounter**. Verse 5 says that arguments must be cast down. Most of our strongholds began by subscribing to lies in order to justify its beginning in our life. Those lies must be displaced with truth from the Bible. There must also be an **allegiance encounter**. These arguments and lies exalt themselves against the knowledge of God (verse 5) and force us into a decision about our perception of who God is and what part He has in our life. It is important that there be nothing between me and the Savior in order to live in liberty. It also may be necessary to have a **power encounter** in order to bring every one of these lies, arguments, and reasonings in the captivity of Christ (verse 5). This encounter requires that I stand in the power of Jesus' name and His blood to overcome the enemy that has dug into my life and plans to keep the grounds he has taken.

James 4:7-10 is a familiar passage to the seasoned believer. It details for us the process by which we break into freedom from the power and influence of the enemy. My first step toward freedom from a stronghold is to submit myself to God. This entails an honest confession of my inability to free my own heart. I must not hide in shame from God as Adam did in the garden. I must run to Him and plead His mercy and forgiveness while trusting Him for deliverance. This means that I come into agreement with God about my sin. I don't minimize nor exaggerate the strength of the stronghold in my life. I must see my sin as God sees it. At this beginning point toward deliverance, I will use God's Word to determine God's will in the matter. Once I have determined God's will, I will then agree with God about it and commit to do His will in it.

The second step is to resist the devil. I can either submit to God or to the devil but not to both. If I choose to submit to God, I must be prepared for a battle simply because Satan will not give up ground that he is in possession of easily. This will require that I die to myself since heretofore I have lived for myself under the influence of the stronghold. It important to remove as much from my life (and home) as gives grounds to the devil. It is curious how many Christians have fetishes in their home that demons have attached themselves to.

We once had demonic manifestations, turmoil, strife, and deception among our pastoral staff in a church that I pastored. I later realized that one of our pastors had preached in a South Sea island and had brought back wooden masks that had been used in pagan settings. He had hung these on the wall in his office at church. Once the fetishes were gone, there was no more problem among staff for as long as I remained at that church.

I knew a man that had been a sailor in his younger years. In his travels, he had purchased an idol carved from rosewood called a Fasting Buddha. The idol was the image of an emaciated man seated with a walking stick in his hand. In talking of his years as a sailor, one of the most common subjects that he talked about was how hungry he often was in those years as a young man at sea, never making a connection to the fetish representing hunger that he had attached himself to. In fact, it seemed as if he felt hungry for the rest of his life.

Resisting the devil includes ridding oneself of any items that may have a connection to the stronghold. Soul ties must be broken. Fetishes must be destroyed. Don't set the stage nor give ground to the enemy. So many times, I have seen Christians moved upon by the Holy Spirit to become free from bondage. Often, this process began with cleaning out their house of dark objects that fed the stronghold.

The third step is to expect by faith the presence and power of God to work in my life. James 4:8 ensures that God will draw near to me. He said that He would so I will embrace that truth by faith. A common fear of the defeated believer is that he will be rejected by God thus sealing his hopelessness. But God is a God of hope. He drives out despair and defeat by filling us with His presence. I will place myself in whatever setting, surround myself with whatever people, and put myself into whatever environment I need in order to resist the devil, draw near to God and experience His presence in my life.

I must then ask myself probing questions at this point. The only way to please God is by believing Him in faith (Hebrews 11:6). Am I expecting deliverance from the finger of God? Am I believing God to show Himself strong on my behalf (2 Chronicles 16:9)? Am I confessing my sin? Am I praising the Worthy One? Am I cleaning my house, my heart, and my mind?

A stronghold will be known to be gone when a doubleminded person becomes a single minded, focused person. Don't give up or become intimidated by the strength of the stronghold. Keep resisting, drawing near, and believing. One day, the enemy's fortress in your life will come crashing down.

Generational Sins
Chapter 13

Tom was descended from a family of preachers. His grandfather was a preacher and church planter. His father and uncles were preachers. Tom approached me one day with a problem of lust. He was overwhelmed at times with unnatural desire for other women. He had a beautiful wife and children, he was a Bible teacher in our church, and he loved the Lord but he couldn't get past this ever-present temptation of lust. I questioned him about pornography but that was not a part of his life. I could not find any basis for this powerful drive that threatened who he professed to be. Several years after this conversation, Tom fell into adultery, lost his family and job, and had to move to a new location to begin again. It was some time after this that he found out that this was generational sin as both his father and uncles (preachers/pastors) had been in regular adulterous affairs during their ministering years and had passed on that vulnerability to Tom. It turned out to be a family affair.

In Adam's fall in the garden, the genetics of the human race were damaged. Our spiritual DNA suffered a permanent fracturing that continues until we die. The entire human race fell in Adam. Sin entered through one man's fall and was programmed into the DNA of the entire population. Sin is not like breathing in a spore or bacteria that makes us spiritually sick. We are programmed with a propensity to sin. It comes naturally to us. Since Jesus was not born of man, he did not have this corruption in Him but all others do.

Generational sin takes advantage of the fact that past failures into sin are programmed within us through family ties. So often, the negative side of life is passed to us in birth. Have you ever seen some parental characteristic manifested in yourself and wished it was not there?

Once I was visiting with a young woman whose mother I had known for several years. She had certain mannerisms that I had noticed in her mother years before. I made the comment that she was like her mother in some ways. Her eyes flashed at me for a moment and she spat out, "I'm trying not to be like her."

There are certain aspects of our life that were handed to us genetically. Psalm 51:5 states that we were conceived with a sin nature. It is not what I do that is offensive to God's holiness; it is more of what I am within my own natural makeup. This reality can be seen in adopted children reverting to life styles, attitudes, gestures, etc. of natural family members in spite of a complete change in environment. Spiritual genetic traits can be carried and manifested no matter what the environment. We find in the early pages of the Bible that Adam rebelled and his son Cain rebelled. Noah's son Ham rebelled and his son Canaan rebelled also. Abraham lied about his wife, Sarah, and his son Isaac repeated the sin with his wife. David's lust was multiplied a thousand times in his son Solomon. The trend holds true throughout history.

A woman once asked me why God had whole villages killed in the Old Testament. It was mainly to cut off the generational sin lines in those families. God has given several warnings concerning generational sins. Exodus 20:5 states that God will visit the sin of the fathers on the children to the third and fourth generations. This is repeated in Numbers 14:17-18. It is also repeated in Exodus 34:6-7 and Deuteronomy 5:8-10. God does not punish children for their parents' sins but rather He deals with the children about sins they have picked up from their parents. Children are vulnerable and moldable. They learn a lot of sin at home. God is determined to cut off the chain of sin in a family. It may take Him three or four generations but He is determined to do it. He is willing to cut off and forgive generational sin according to Leviticus 26:40-42.

Generational sins can be easily traced. A father is violent and so is his son as an adult. An alcoholic now passes that genetic vulnerability to their offspring. A parent is unfaithful to their spouse and later find their adult children following the same behavior. Some are now even saying that homosexuality can be a genetic disposition although the jury is still out on the science of that one. Depression, anger, prejudice, sexual sins and much other vulnerability is easily passed down.

I once dealt with a demonized young man in our church and identified twelve different named spirits operating in his life. One of those spirits had been operating in his family for several generations. When questioned and held to the truth, that demonic spirit took responsibility for causing every sibling in that family to divorce for four generations spanning over a hundred years.

Biblical accounts are plenty in light of generational sins. Abraham rebelled against God's standard in his sin with Hagar. His grandson Jacob rebelled and stole his brother's birthright through deception. Sarah pushed Ishmael out as did her daughter-in-law, Rebekah, when she pushed her son Esau out of his inheritance. When Benjamin killed his mother in childbirth, the curse was broken. Abraham had a wife but also had an affair with Hagar. His grandson Jacob treated his first wife, Leah, as a prostitute. Judah, Jacob's son, engaged in an affair with a prostitute. Jacob had contempt for his brother Esau and lied to his father in order to cheat his brother Esau. Jacob's sons would also lie to him about their brother Joseph. Later, repentance and forgiveness broke this trend of sin. David committed adultery with Bathsheba and had her husband murdered. David's son raped his own sister (David's sexual sin returning) and one of his other sons killed the son who raped the sister (David's sin of murder returning).

I once read a study out of UCLA done on adopted children. The study was done from 1924 to 1947. Children of convicts were shown to have a greater vulnerability to repeating the actions of the parents than those whose parents were law abiding people. Children of convicts were more likely to break the law. If natural parents had three or more convictions, 20% of the sons had one or more convictions.

One of the most interesting studies done followed two family lines through several generations. In 1900, A. E, Winship published "Jukes-Edwards: A study in Education and Heredity". In this study (which some disagree with), Winship follows the families of Max Jukes and Jonathan Edwards, the puritan preacher. The skinny summary of this study states that Mr. Jukes had 1200 descendants. 130 of them were convicted criminals. 310 of them were professional paupers. 400 were seriously injured or physically degenerated by sinful living. 60 were professional thieves or pickpockets. 17 turned out to be murderers. Only 20 of the descendants learned a trade, 10 of them learned their trade in prison.

The family of Jonathan Edwards was quite different. Of 400 descendants, 100 of them became preachers, missionaries, or teachers of theology. 100 became professors. 100 became lawyers and judges. 60 became doctors. 14 became college professors. The trend in these two families is glaringly evident.

No one is doomed to practice generational sin but there must be a generation that breaks the bondage in a blood line. Nehemiah 1:4-10 details the kind of repentance and prayer to confess and break generational sins patterns. Questions should be asked by everyone with a family. Where am I vulnerable? Where is my spouse vulnerable? Where will my children be weak? We are a part of a people with weaknesses that can be passed from generation to generation. This generational curse can be broken by God's power. Jesus said all power in heaven and earth is given to Him (Matthew 28:18). All parents, including adoptive parents should take authority over the enemy's place in their children's lives. The truth is, if a parent does not respond to God and take responsibility for their sins, their children may have to.

How are these ties broken? First, the generational sins must be identified. What sins of the parents are the children repeating? These will not be difficult to see since there will be a pattern established. Once this sin or sins is identified, it must be repented of no matter what form it takes or how irregular its occurrence. Someone with spiritual authority must stand against it in confession and repentance. There should be a renunciation of the sin with the repentance. Examples of identifying with generational sins are found in Nehemiah 1:4-9; Jeremiah 14:20; and Daniel 9:1-19.

The warfare must be done by the power of Jesus' name and the blood of the cross. Take authority in Jesus' name and bind it from your loved one's life. It may not be as easy as a simple prayer. Sometimes the devil has had his hand in the family for several generations and will not relinquish that authority quickly but, greater is He who is in you ...

Soul Ties
Chapter 14

Some years ago, God blew through our church one weekend in a deep revival that changed everything about the church. For several years the influence of that revival directed the church's ministry (see my book **Walking in the Wind**). In the midst of that revival, our church did the warfare through prayer to close and take possession of the local abortion clinic that was less than a half mile from our church building. It was the greatest point of darkness in our county. For years there had picketing, letters written to politicians, and other efforts made to close the clinic. None of these were successful but prayer closed the clinic. Abortion would no longer be legally practiced in that part of our state. In the following months, a strange phenomenon began to occur. In the eighteen months following our taking possession of the abortion clinic and converting it into a Sunday School building, among the families in our congregation, twenty-one babies died in the womb. It was so common that the word began to spread that if a woman became pregnant, she should leave our church or else the baby would die before it was born. There was no explanation that I could give for it until one day, just out of the blue, the Holy Spirit showed me that this was a result of our connection to the abortion clinic. Evidently, we had established a soul tie with the work of the clinic and instead of babies dying in the womb in the clinic through the abortion process, they began to die in the womb of church members. I immediately determined to sever this soul tie. I called together thirty of our strongest prayer warriors and one evening we met together at the church building and severed the tie with the spirit of death that had attached itself to our church body. In the years that I remained pastor after that night of prayer, we lost only two babies in the womb. Both were miscarriages of the same woman who had a history of miscarriage.

A soul tie is a spiritual bond established through relationships that has influence from one person to the other. It is like a spiritual umbilical cord from a mother's body to an infant in the womb or it may be visualized as a pipeline transferring spiritual influence from one entity to another.

There are both good and bad soul ties. Biblically, this truth is demonstrated in words like: knit, cleave, join, and bind.

There are multiple examples in the Bible of positive soul ties. These are soul ties between friends like Jonathan and David who became one in spirit (1 Samuel 18:1). Soul ties are established between a parent and child as with Jacob and Benjamin whose lives were bound up together (Genesis 44:30). A link can certainly be established between a leader and followers as when David's supporters stayed with him (2 Samuel 20:2). A soul tie is established between a husband and wife and creates oneness as they cleave to each other (Genesis 2:24). Even between God and His people a soul tie is established as His people hold fast to Him (Deuteronomy 10:20). There are many good soul ties established between followers of Jesus as they are united in love (Colossians 2:2, 19). These soul ties establish healthy connections of spiritual influence, power, and oneness.

Just as there are positive and healthy soul ties, there are also dangerous soul ties that can be established such as the one that we unknowingly allowed to form between our church and the abortion clinic. God warns us against people who are trouble makers (Romans 16:17-18) and who divide, damage, and sabotage because of potential soul ties that can be formed and unwanted influence or action that could come into our life. We are told not to be unequally yoked with unbelievers (2 Corinthians 6:14). The sexually impure are to be avoided (1 Corinthians 5:9-13) as are the sowers of discord that God hates (Proverbs 6:19). These types of people whose influence and actions are undesirable to the Kingdom of God are to be avoided lest an unhealthy soul tie is formed and we begin to take on characteristics of the enemy of God. We are warned of a soul tie to the world and clinging to its values and systems (Joshua 23:12). We see the soul tie danger with a violent, immoral person in Genesis 34:2-3. To give oneself to a prostitute is to create a soul tie of oneness with them (1 Corinthians 6:16).

Jackie was a middle-aged woman who came to me very troubled. She had grown up under a very dominating mother who could never be pleased. Although her mother had died, Jackie continued to live under the pressure of pleasing her mother with her life. She thought it foolish to still be under the influence that had made her childhood and young adult years so miserable. I had learned sometime before this conversation that even though a dominating, abusive parent may die, Satan can usurp authority and take advantage of the natural soul tie between a parent and child and represent the dead parent on the giving side of the soul tie. She voiced a desire to be free from this cloud that seemed to cover her still. I suggested two things to her.

First, she needed to forgive her mother for the abuse. Write her a letter voicing every feeling and emotion that you have had to deal with. Verbalize them on paper, then, write your forgiveness to her. Bring the letter to me as a representative of a parental figure and I will destroy it.

Secondly, renounce any lingering influence in Jesus' name and embrace deliverance from this connection to darkness. Jackie did both of these within a week. She brought me her letter to her mother sealed in an envelope and I burned it without opening it. She began to experience a new freedom that had never been part of her life and lived in that freedom for the rest of her life. The soul tie had been severed.

Do you have friends who seem to have a strange ability to influence you in ways you know are not suitable for a Christian? Do you have parents, alive or dead, that were abusive, domineering, or hurtful in some way and continue to have influence over you? Perhaps it's time to renounce your connection with this darkness and sever the soul tie, asking that Jesus now be the power that influences you instead of the negative one that has been in your life.

Curses and their Cure
Chapter 15

James and Natalie was a young married couple in our church. I had known them since their teenage years. Both of their families were faithful Christians with a working knowledge of God's Word. James and Natalie had fallen in love, followed Biblical courtship principles, and I had married them. Now, several years had passed and they found themselves unable to have children. There seemed to be no medical reason for this barrenness.

Upon a day, the Holy Spirit revealed to James that he was under a curse concerning children. He knew little to nothing about demonic curses but had the deepest impression that this was the couple's problem. In his early days as a coach, a mother of a child he was coaching became very upset and belligerent with James and declared to him that he would never have children of his own to raise. He thought nothing of the threat and simply noted that another upset parent had voiced her anger toward him. Now, it all came back to him. He approached me about the situation. We happened to have a visiting evangelist preaching at our church at that time who was very knowledgeable in spiritual warfare.

When the possible curse was mentioned to him, the evangelist readily agreed and called for a time of prayer to break this curse. Several of us gathered with James and Natalie to pray over them. In the name of Jesus and by the power of the blood of the cross, we canceled the curse and lifted the ban against conception. Today, James and Natalie have three children, all of them saved and following Jesus.

The concept of curses seems to be a strange idea to most Christians. It is reminiscent of fictional movies and books conjuring up scenes of Voodoo and witchcraft, black cats and flying broomsticks. The reality of curses is established Biblically to be a real threat to Christians. Those believers who are walking in the "power of His might" in their spiritual authority are a constant threat to Satan's kingdom. They are displacing darkness with light, hatred with love, and sin with righteousness. Ancient pagan cultures that practiced dark magic with the assistance of the demonic powers available to them eventually had descendants from their areas to immigrate to the U.S.A. They came from Europe, the Black Forest, Africa, Caribbean Islands, Russia, Scandinavia, and England's Druids.

Many of them brought their dark powers with them.

Not everyone who has angry words hurled at them are under a demonic curse. There are curses that attach themselves to certain sins by which we curse ourselves. Even God revealed that those who rob Him of tithes and offerings have put themselves under a curse (Malachi 3:9). Cain was placed under a curse because he murdered his brother Abel (Genesis 4:11). Those sins create open doors to allow evil spirits to set up legal grounds to operate from. I have known churches to be under a curse. I know of one church that has lost several pastors and staff members to adultery or sexual perversion spanning a period of decades. Some churches have been plagued with spirits of contention, racism, or other dominant sins. I once pastored a church with the greatest concentration of cancer that I had ever been aware of. It seemed as though nearly everyone in the church either had cancer or was recovering from it.

When our church took possession of our local abortion clinic and made it a building for Bible teaching, Satanists in full robed garb with torches marched around our church building at night casting curses on our congregation. They came into the services to curse the people as they sat in the sanctuary. We cancelled every curse thrown our way.

Bobby found himself in my office one day bothered by demonic spirits who manifested themselves in violence. In retracing his past in order to find the open door that welcomed this sort of spiritual wickedness into his life he confessed that he had once murdered someone and no one had ever suspected him. This opened the door for other sin to come in to his life and now he found himself under the domination of these dark spirits. Deliverance came shortly after this conversation.

Most curses are placed upon one's life by words. James 3:6 says the tongue is set on fire by hell. Psalm 109:17 says that curses are pronounced. Balaam was hired to curse the people of Israel as they traveled through the wilderness to the Promised Land. Too many times a frustrated parent will hurl a curse at one of their children, "I hope that one day you have children that will give you the same grief that you give me." Many times, I see Christians cursing their own life with negative confession about bad luck, adversity, and other life obstacles. Words are powerful instruments both for righteousness in giving blessings and for darkness in pronouncing curses.

It has been demonstrated in history that curses can go back multiple generations in families. There has been much written about the Kennedy curse in American history. Some families seem to deal with adversity or particular sins for several generations. When curses are lifted and broken, it should be done back to four or five generations just to be safe and also to protect the generations to come.

How does one cancel curses believed to be placed upon them or their church? It is done through prayer and the power of the blood of the cross. The process put forth in the scripture is twofold.

One is to displace curses with blessings. When the good hand of God is upon one, curses have a difficult time exercising any power over the blessings of God. Balaam was not able to pronounce a curse upon Israel because they were blessed by God (Numbers 22:12). Nehemiah stated that God had turned the curse into blessing (Nehemiah 13:2). To pronounce the blessings of God can many times displace the power of a curse.

The second way to deal with a curse is to stand in the authority of Jesus Christ and return the curse to its source.

He loved to pronounce a curse – may it come back on him. Psalms 109:17

His mischief will return upon his own head. Psalm 7:16

Hear, O our God; for we are despised: and turn their reproach upon their own head. Nehemiah 4:4

The nations have sunk down in the pit which they have made; in the net which they hid, their own foot has been caught. Psalms 9:15

Let the net that he hid ensnare him. Psalm 35:8

I would pray a simple powerful prayer of release from any curses over my children, my church, my family, my finances and other areas of life that may seem to be vulnerable. If there were no curses, nothing has been lost.

I stand against and cancel any curse planed upon my life back to the fourth generation and send the curse back to where it came from in the name of Jesus Christ and by the power of the blood of the cross.

Territorial Spirits
Chapter 16

Daniel was a man of great prayer and fasting. On one occasion of prayer, he fasted while praying for twenty-one days, waiting for an answer (Daniel 10). When the messenger finally arrived with God's answer, the messenger told Daniel that God had heard him on the first day of his praying but a territorial spirit, the prince of the kingdom of Persia, had restrained him to the point that Michael, the archangel, was dispatched to fight the demonic spirit and allow the answer to reach Daniel.

Several years ago, I decided to do some spiritual mapping of the region that our church was in. I wanted to displace the darkness with light but in order to do this, I needed to know what the governing spirits were. I spent many weeks in our public library going over the history of our area and establishing the source of the dominant sins in our region. A territorial spirit will be responsible for the dominant sins in a geographical area. It is not unusual for a region to have the same dominant sins for generations. The contract with these territorial spirits is usually renewed each year through some festival or public celebration in honor of that particular dominant sin.

I found that our region, on the east bank of the Mississippi River had four dominant spirits controlling the culture in which we lived. At least one of these dated back over 500 years to native American activity.

The first regional problem that I found I called the "*Redneck Syndrome*". It found its beginnings in our area to be through the migration of the Chickasaw Indians. This syndrome's dominant characteristics involved the family. It manifested itself in our day through the husband/father in the home leaving the responsibilities of the home almost exclusively to the wife. She took care of the house (tipi), the children, the cooking, and most other duties. The husband spent much of his time with his friends talking about the latest 4WD (horse), biggest kill, catch, or conquest. The young braves of the Chickasaw tribe had passed down this behavior through 500 years of history. As I studied the social and religious beliefs of this tribe, I learned that they had migrated from Mexican territory because of war. They decided to move east to get away from the aggression of the Apache and Commanche tribes. The process that they used in the migration involved a sanctified rod and their religious oracle. Each night this oracle placed the rod standing up in the ground. The direction it had fallen by morning is the direction that they moved. For many months, they followed the rod's direction that pointed eastward every morning. Once they had crossed the Mississippi River into the present state of Mississippi, the stick never fell again and they remained to become a large tribe stretching across Mississippi, Alabama, and Tennessee. They sacrificed blood offerings of animals in the woods, ate the heart of their enemies, and drank from the skulls of their enemies. Their male treatment of women eventually translated itself into the drinking, hunting, fishing, and sporting culture of much of the South today. I saw it in many of the husbands attending church with us.

The second regional problem was the "*Racial Hatred Syndrome*". Our church's influence in ministry stretched across five counties just south of Memphis, Tennessee. Much of the rapid growth in our county happened because of racial tension in Memphis that caused "white flight" into our area. At one time, I counted fourteen churches that had moved their entire congregations across the state line into our county in order to escape changing neighborhoods and racial diversity. Most congregations in our county, including ours, was fully white. Memphis is an angry town where Martin Luther King, James Meredith, and other black leaders had been killed. At the time that I was studying this, the grand wizard of the KKK in our area lived within walking distance of our church. There had been much racial hatred, abuse, and murder in our region for nearly two hundred years. General Nathan Bedford Forest had sold slaves in his slave market eight miles from our church. This regional sin translated into our churches with the standard prejudice that accompanies racism and resulted in most congregations in our county, including ours, being fully white. Sunday was the most segregated day of the week for us.

The third regional problem was the "*Musical Vacuum Syndrome*". Memphis, where most of our members worked, shopped, and were entertained, is a music center. Some of the greatest names in the music world found their beginning there. Elvis, B.B. King, Staxx Music, Jerry Lee Lewis (he lived in our county), Carl Perkins, Johnny Cash, and many more got their start in our area. Rock and roll,

Blues, Rockabilly, alternative, and other styles originated there. The result was a total vacuum of Christian music in the air. There were many stations of every sort broadcasting everyday around the clock but not one Christian station was allowed in. When there was an opening for a station to come on the air, the FCC gave the space to PBS rather than to any Christian entity. As a result, there was a vacuum of praise music in the air. Since we know that Satan is atmospheric (prince of the power of the air) he controlled the atmospheric worship, or lack thereof, over our population.

    A fourth regional problem was the "*Corruption Syndrome*". This corruption of local government traced itself back to bootleggers, hose thieves, cattle thieves, and other outlaws hiding out in the forests of the river bluffs and bribing public officials to turn their head to their crimes. Saloons had once dominated most street corners of our county seat and other settlements. Illegal gambling halls, bordellos, casinos, stills for moonshine, and massage parlors had resulted in generations of corrupt politicians, pay offs, cover ups, and various elements of darkness. This syndrome had been entrenched for so long that it was openly displayed from the law enforcement leaders to mayors and city government.

Once these territorial strongholds were established, the work of the church was to displace these demonic rulers with counter actions to break up their domination over the region. I am grateful to say that in the following years much of this darkness had been broken up by the body of Christ.

By the time I was reassigned by the Lord to another region, there was a strong Christian radio station broadcasting around the clock over our area cancelling the music vacuum syndrome.

We had elected Christian government leaders, judges, mayors, city government, and law enforcement leaders that changed the whole corruption syndrome. Government officials now led in prayer breakfasts for the citizens, worship events, and had prayer at their gatherings.

Our church had become racially mixed and open. This was a real test for our church back in that day but is a standard operating value now. This helped break up the racial hatred syndrome.

Our church underwent a strong revival, especially among the men of our church which reset the care that they showed their wives and children. Jesus became the priority of their lives thus breaking up the redneck syndrome.

We would have never been able to break these geographical strongholds had the territorial spirits not been identified. There is much for Christians to learn about these dominating territorial spirits.

It is important to learn the point of entry that these spirits use as an open door to set up their governing work. We know from Genesis 1:26 that Satan usurped the dominion of Adam in the earth by beguiling Eve and causing Adam to follow her into sin. This led to lying, deceit, jealousy, and murder. A progressive work of domination began. Satan eventually established a covering over the entire earth (Isaiah 25:7) that began in the garden of Eden. He became the atmospheric god of this world. 1 John 4:3 reveals to us that the spirit of antichrist (Antichrist will be Satan in the flesh) is already functioning in the earth.

The demonic kingdom of darkness is regimented into levels of spirits like a well-organized army. Most people are only bothered by ground level spirits simply because they do not think in terms of spiritual coverings of darkness. Most don't know that it is the ground level spirits that are causing them problems.

According to Ephesians 6:12, there are four levels of demonic power operating on the earth. There are first the **Ground-Level** spirits (spiritual wickedness) who deal with individuals. These are those identified in Mark 5 with Jesus' encounter with the demoniac among the tombs. I have identified over sixty of these spirits by name in dealing with demonized individuals. They usually either take on the name of their sin (like lust, rebellion, etc.) or some proper name that may have roots in darkness from the distant past. I have dealt with names like Romulan, Sicilian, Liza, Ron, Constantine, Judas, Jesus, Legion, Apollo, and Centurion.

Next there are **Middle-Level** spirits (rulers of darkness). These spirits produce dominant features of darkness in an area. Drugs, alcohol, Satanism, adult stores and videos, etc. They provide resources for the sins prompted by the Ground Level spirits.

There are also **High-Level** spirits (powers). These spirits are responsible for the general darkness over an area. These have possibly been entrenched for generations. They help keep a dark covering over a geographical area.

Lastly, there are the powerful **Highest-Level** spirits (principalities). I remember these by noting that they are a prince over a pality. They dominate a territory or even a nation. They are very powerful with much authority. It was this level spirit that Michael the archangel had to deal with in Daniel's day.

In order to break the influence and power of these spirits, it will take the unity of Christians and the help of angels, in some cases, to overcome them. As long as believers are critical, spiteful, and accusing of other Christians and their leaders, these demonic forces are not threatened. The battle must be intentional with well informed and very powerful Christ-like leadership.

Self-Deliverance
Chapter 17

After a number of "power encounters" with demonized people, it was a relief to come to place where we could help someone self-deliver. I had caught enough mucous and vomit in my hands, trashcans, and paper towels to never want to participate in a deliverance session again. Matthew 8:16 uses the words "cast out" in reference to deliverance. It indicates a violent action. This word literally fulfills itself in a power encounter with a demon. It was always nasty and ugly. I knew that most demonization comes from buying into lies from the enemy. I also knew that Jesus had assured us that truth would set us free.

In visiting with Sheila one day, she had told me that her problems began when she decided that resentment toward her mother was justified. As a teenager, she was standing at the sink doing dishes when her mother began to ride her about her behavior. She became so resentful at her mother's attitude that at that moment she became demonized. She knew the exact moment it happened. She had problems with the demonic from that point on until such time that she reached out for help as a young woman. She had embraced the lie that her mother was not understanding, compassionate, or loving. She decided at that point to give herself to resentment, rebellion, and bitterness toward her mother. Her deliverance came when she rejected those lies, renounced the influence of those lies, and embraced the truth that her mother did love her and was worthy of honor. She was never bothered again.

Not everyone is able to reach a point of self-deliverance but many can with some spiritual coaching. Repentance, renunciation, and renewal can bring a person to freedom without the violent tearing and general nastiness of a power encounter. It may take longer to be free as truth is embraced and internalized but it is much more effective. The entry point must be identified and the legal grounds for the presence of the enemy must be removed. Recovering surrendered ground involves repentance of sin, severing of unhealthy soul ties, restitution, and renouncing sin's influence on the life of the demonized one. Many of the demonized ones that I have dealt with had their beginnings of demonization in childhood sexual abuse. Forgiveness of the offender played a great part in maintaining their deliverance.

    Truth is a powerful force in displacing darkness. Once one understands the truth of God about life and godly living, much surrendered territory can be recovered. Learning, embracing, and doing the Word of God will bring a person to the point of realizing that the controlling spirits have left and it really cannot be determined exactly when it happened, only that their legal grounds were removed. The spirits had nothing to stand on and no reason to stay so, they are gone.

Frequently Asked Questions
Chapter 18

How can one know if someone is demonized as opposed to simply having a bad attitude?

There will be manifestations. I ask questions like: Do you hear voices that seem real? Do you ever lose control of your life and it seems as if someone else is in control? Do you have blank times when you can't remember being aware of a certain time frame?

Can demons prevent us from seeing them?

Yes, just like angels.

What about ghosts or seeing people who are dead?

Ghosts are manifestations of demons.

Should I be afraid of demons?

Demons are much like bad kids. They can't always hurt someone but they produce fear and trouble in order to control. The spiritually grounded believer need not be afraid of the demonic.

Are there such things as haunted houses in which demons can dwell in the home through a duration of multiple home owners over the years?

Yes. Once they have grounds to be there, they can stay until forced out. We once lived in a house once where our teenage son was bothered with suicidal thoughts. We found out later that the former occupant of the house had, in fact, committed suicide.

Can demons take on non-human forms?

Certainly, anything an angel can do. I once talked with a woman who was bothered by a demonic spirit on a regular basis in her home, mostly at night. He appeared in the form of a gargoyle and it had raped her several times. She decided not to work toward deliverance for fear of reprisal from this spirit. It was the most bizarre incident I had come across.

Can demons produce illusions outside of themselves as with smells, temperature, or noises?

Yes. They are atmospheric. The first exposure that I had with a demonic spirit was as a young, newly married man. What I remember most about the experience was the icy cold temperature in the room.

Is it common for demonic activity to increase at times?

Yes. Jesus in the wilderness. Jesus in the garden of Gethsemane. I have experienced times of increased attacks during times of fasting and prayer or during times of great spiritual advancement in the church.

Can demons read our mind?

I find no Biblical evidence that demons can read our minds. They have seen humans living life since Adam's day and they can read body language, know our thought patterns and history, and watch our eyes to see what we see. They are very astute at reading an individual knowing human nature as they do.

How should one respond to a "CHANCE" meeting of someone who is demonized?

Bind it up in Jesus' name. For some reason, I can draw out a demonic response from someone without trying. I suppose they know who I am and the damage I have caused their kingdom.

I got on a small plane one night in Boston to fly to Atlanta. A woman got on after me and I thought she was drunk. She was using filthy language, was angry, and her eyes were like fire. She sat across from and behind me. Once she took her seat the vileness began to flow from her mouth out loud. I knew what was happening. The demon is her was bothered by the Jesus in me. I turned in my seat and locked eyes with her. The eyes usually give them away. While holding her gaze (which was penetrating right through me) I bound the spirit up in my heart without saying a word out loud. Once I bound the spirit up by the power of Jesus' name and the blood of the cross, she immediately dropped her head on her chest and went sound to sleep for the rest of the flight. When I left the plane, she was still quiet.

What makes some demons stronger than others?

The ranks of authority given to them.

Are paranormal entities demonic in nature?

Yes.

If paranormal activities are demonic, why would they present useful information to people with psychic abilities who have "spirit guides" that give them information?

Their purpose is to establish legitimacy in order to deceive, confuse, and distract from truth.

Is it wrong to communicate with demons through mediums like Ouija boards, seances, etc.?

Yes. This is divination and the Bible forbids it. Acts 16:16.

Made in the USA
Middletown, DE
20 August 2017